M000033558

# A SEAT AT THE TABLE

*A Generation Reimagining Its Place in the Church*

## SHAWNA SONGER GAINES & TIMOTHY R. GAINES

BEACON HILL PRESS
OF KANSAS CITY

Copyright 2012
by Timothy R. Gaines, Shawna Songer Gaines,
and Beacon Hill Press of Kansas City

ISBN 978-0-8341-2835-4

Printed in the
United States of America

Cover Design: Arthur Cherry
Inside Design: Sharon Page

All Scripture quotations not otherwise designated are from the *Holy Bible, New International Version*® (NIV 2011®). Copyright © 1973, 1978, 1984, 2011 by Biblica, Inc.™ Used by permission. All rights reserved worldwide.

**Library of Congress Cataloging-in-Publication Data**
Gaines, Shawna Songer, 1984-
    A seat at the table : a generation reimagining its place in the church / Shawna Songer Gaines and Timothy R. Gaines.
        p. cm.
    Includes bibliographical references and index.
    ISBN 978-0-8341-2835-4 (pbk. : alk. paper)
  1. Church.  2. Intergenerational relations—Religious aspects—Christianity.
3. Church attendance.  4. Hospitality—Religious aspects—Christianity.
I. Gaines, Timothy R., 1981-  II. Title.
    BV640.G35 2012
    262.0084'2—dc23
                                                                                    2012020112

10  9  8  7  6  5  4  3  2  1

For our grandparents, who have through their faithfulness
given us a seat at the table:

Ray and Joy Bircher
Ray and Evie Gaines
Joe and Geneva McIntyre
Estey and Joyce Songer

# CONTENTS

# INTRODUCTION

THE FIRST TIME we ever tasted oyster stuffing was at Thanksgiving with some friends. We had been lifelong stuffing traditionalists and were pretty sure that nothing that had once lived in saltwater belonged on the Thanksgiving table—but when you get together with friends who grew up in different families with different traditions, oyster stuffing is what you get. And really, it didn't matter all that much to us. We loved the company enough to overlook mollusks next to the cranberry sauce.

We had been gathering together for Thanksgiving for a few years, a group of graduate students and their spouses who supported them through seminary by working real jobs. Some were friends from college we reunited with in seminary, and others were friends we had met once we started our seminary studies. Nonetheless, we became a family with a profound sense of care and commitment to one another. This year Thanksgiving was at our house.

Being a group of idealists with no real commitments after graduation, our group conversations usually turned toward the way we would all be together again one day planting the perfect church. We had all grown up in church, we were all passionate about serving the church, and we had all taken the wonderfully insane steps of moving thousands of miles from everything we knew to pursue training toward that end. We were also in various stages of preparing for ordination, which in our minds was mostly sacred but partly bureaucratic. I had been delayed yet another year on a bookkeeping technicality, the result of another move to a new area. I wasn't alone.

"I'm not going to be ordained either," said Rick. I knew by the tone in his voice that he wasn't talking about a bookkeeping technicality but that there was something deeper under the surface. I had known Rick for several years after we met in seminary, where he quickly struck me as someone who had a lot to offer. He was engaging, intelligent, passionate, and different enough from me to make him interesting.

"You too, huh?" I asked, hoping he would open up a bit more about what was going on with him. I expected that we would talk shop for a little while and air our complaints about some kind of hoop we needed to jump through. What he actually said, though, changed the direction of the conversation and made an indelible mark on my memory.

"I just don't know anymore," he said quietly. "I don't know that I'm going to pursue ordination anymore." We were all a bit stunned and felt as if a thick, heavy blanket had fallen over us, making it hard to see and hear clearly. Rick went on to tell us about his most recent experience in his pursuit of ministry, dealing mainly with a hard conversation he had a few months earlier with an older pastor who had questioned his intentions.

"Honestly," he said flatly, "I think this was just the straw that broke the camel's back. I didn't know it was broken for a while, but it was."

In what he told us that night, Rick took us through his journey of wondering if there was a place for him in the church. "I was a zealous kid," he remembered, laughing a bit as he filled out his thought. "I was afraid all my friends were going to hell because I wasn't a good-enough witness. I was *that* kid."

"In some ways, you still are," someone said.

"Yeah, maybe. I mean, I'm still zealous, but I just don't know if the church has room for me or not."

Rick went on to tell us that he sensed God calling him to ministry at an early age and how he was outspoken about his calling. The trouble was that his hair was long, he had a piercing or two, and he played guitar a lot—listening to music that most of the folks in his church found difficult to stomach. "I was an alternative kid," he said, "but I was a really *zealous* alternative kid."

As he began to express his call to ministry, Rick said that initially he didn't receive much support from the leaders in his church, not because he wasn't gifted for the task but because he didn't look the part. "You won't be a pastor with a haircut like that," he remembers a pastor saying to him once.

"I thought I could put up with the snide comments," Rick explained. "I thought this was just part of the game. I had to pay my dues, and as soon as I had done that, I could begin to exert a little influence and make some changes—but I probably couldn't do that until I was in my forties."

Once he was old enough to take on his first part-time ministry assignments, Rick hoped to find a mentor who could help him into ministry, but he sensed that his age and alternative look made older pastors suspicious of his presence in the church. "It was as if they would be willing to let me work the hours," he remembered in some honest moments, "but there was no way they would ever turn the church over to me."

Just before he was to be considered for ordination, Rick had a particularly rough ordination interview with a group of pastors who were unsatisfied with his responses to their questions. "It wasn't that I couldn't answer questions about where to find certain passages in the Bible but that I was using different passages than whatever they were looking for. I thought I was a good Bible student."

We all thought so too. If we were honest, we would have to admit that we were all probably a bit jealous that Rick had scored so much higher on the Bible entrance exams to seminary than the rest of us—probably combined.

"And I guess that was it," he confided. "I still believe in the church. I still believe in holiness. I still believe in God's redemption. But I'm just not finding a place for me."

After the guest rooms were empty and the smell of oysters dissipated, we got to thinking about that conversation. Why was it that

> RICK SAID THAT INITIALLY HE DIDN'T RECEIVE MUCH SUPPORT FROM THE LEADERS IN HIS CHURCH, NOT BECAUSE HE WASN'T GIFTED FOR THE TASK BUT BECAUSE HE DIDN'T LOOK THE PART.

someone who was so gifted, who had so much to offer to the church, felt there wasn't room for him? It wasn't as if he was ready to give up on his faith. It wasn't as if he had planned to leave the church for a while—but it was more that the church didn't have a place for him. It got us thinking about the others we have known over time who have also struggled with this same sense of placelessness when it came to the church.

Most of the time, the people who came to mind were young, and most of the time it was their youth that seemed to be the greatest hindrance to their finding a place in the church. They thought differently, dressed differently, communicated differently, and it was all just a bit too different to fit in at church. It wasn't that they weren't willing to be discipled or that they thought the church needed to somehow conform to their personal theology—it seemed that even as confessing Christ as Lord they couldn't find a seat at the table. Given the options, many had chosen to quietly disappear from the church.

There are several things about this that gave us pause and caused us grief, one being the fact that when these young people were disappearing, so were the gifts they had to offer to the church for the sake of the kingdom of God. There was so much they could give, so much energy, passion, creativity, imagination, and—contrary to what is often thought about the younger generation—so much commitment they were prepared to give. But in the face of frustration, of being cut out because they don't seem to fit, they often took their gifts and took their leave of the church.

It could be the case that when we hear stories like Rick's it's a matter of young energy impetuously bumping into the rest of the world. It could be that this is the way youth have encountered the world for generations. It could be that young people like Rick are living proof of the stereotype of the YouTube generation and that they need constant laud and attention and are unable to take constructive critique. Comedy writers have been poking fun at the stereotype for several years now. One of the more memorable examples is a fresh-faced twenty-something with a nice suit, shoulder-length hair, and a newly minted business school diploma appearing on the NBC sit-com *30 Rock*. "I don't want this job unless I'm going to be constantly praised," he arrogantly tells his potential employer during a job interview. "And I'm not going to cut my hair."

We might be far more inclined to chalk up Rick's story to that kind of an explanation if it weren't for the data that sociologists are giving us, demonstrating that young people in North America are far less likely now to meaningfully engage the church than their parents were.[1] And as we look around in the churches we've served, we've seen that the data rings true in the real world. Young people are having a difficult time finding a place in the church.

AS WE LOOK AROUND IN THE CHURCHES WE'VE SERVED, WE'VE SEEN THAT THE DATA RINGS TRUE IN THE REAL WORLD. YOUNG PEOPLE ARE HAVING A DIFFICULT TIME FINDING A PLACE IN THE CHURCH.

This book comes in response to what we encountered that night around the Thanksgiving table and our concern that North American young people are not finding a place in the Body of Christ. Since hearing Rick's story that night, we've been pressed to engage other young people who have a lot to offer and ask them why they have either stayed with the church or why they've left. Ultimately, the major question underlying all of these stories is this: *Is there a place for me in the church?*

In the stories we've heard while writing this book, some themes have emerged that have become the topic of many of the chapters. We've engaged these themes as young pastors who are disquieted by the growing sociological trends that show young people exiting the church, not necessarily because we want to return the church to some kind of glorious reinstatement of social and political power but because we sense a profound loss in this trend, both for those who have left the church and for the church itself.

For those who have left, we mourn that they are no longer receiving the same gifts that we have received time and again—the gifts that can be given only by saints and the grace of God—the stories, the hope, the healing, the fellowship with God's people that have long sustained and transformed us. And we also mourn for the church, which, like a father awaiting the return of a prodigal child, wonders, longs, worries, and asks where it all went wrong and why young people won't come around much anymore.

This is a project for those who are wondering if there is a place for them in the church. It's also a project for those who are on the "other side" of the sociological or generational divide and are wondering if their church can make space for young people to be vital and contributing members of the body.

Of course, there are some real questions begging for answers along the way: Should young people have to work at finding a place in the church? Is there a time when it's just not worth trying anymore? How should you engage the church if it seems the church is not offering a welcome? This book hopes to explore those questions and what it means to find a place in the church, to find a seat at the table. We want to better understand the reasons for our sense of disconnection, to ask hard questions about the role of church in our faith, to be honest about our own participation in the age of suspicion, and to seek ways to engage in faithful conversations with our worshiping communities that bring us into closer alignment with God's vision for the Kingdom.

We begin with the presupposition that the wideness of Christ's mercy is a gift that can never be repaid. We begin with the idea that God loves this world and that His mission to this world is one of redemption and healing, salvation and sanctification, and that if the church is going to join in that mission, it cannot turn away from a generation seeking a place at the table. Scripture affirms that while we were still sinners, Christ died for us (Romans 5:8).

Yet in the church today there seems to be an increasing suspicion among brothers and sisters regarding who is in and who is out of the scope of Christian orthodoxy and that the wideness of Christ's mercy is being narrowed, leaving young people without a place. Younger Christians who have largely grown up in a postmodern culture do not see postmodernity as an argument to be had but as a reality of life and culture that cannot be altogether incongruent with Christianity. But many Christians were raised in the height of modernity and have struggled with this reality as it grates against—and at times threatens—the modern worldview from which they see their faith.

In the wake of this generational dynamic, many twenty- and thirty-something Christians who have big dreams and visions for what love and redemption ought to look like find themselves placeless within the modern church in North America. Though many in the church are concerned about this dynamic, we are going to suggest that without malice or intent the church continues telling young people how much they are wanted but is not offering a genuine welcome.

IT'S OUR INTENT TO ADDRESS BOTH GENERATIONS WITH SOME OBSERVATIONS AND HOPEFUL SUGGESTIONS FOR WAYS PAST THE DYNAMIC OF GENERATIONAL SUSPICION.

Inasmuch as this dynamic involves at least two parties, it is important to discuss the ways in which not only the modern generation but also the postmodern generation need to assume new postures in order to become a more faithful image of God's kingdom. It's our intent to address both generations with some observations and hopeful suggestions for ways past the dynamic of generational suspicion.

There have been entirely enough books written to explain the shift from modernity to postmodernity and consequently make the case for a Christian engagement in postmodern culture. This book will not attempt to rehash this argument, because we assume that no one needs to be convinced that a paradigm shift is taking place between generations. We don't assume that we need to take a posture of opposition against postmodernity or against modernity, because we don't assume that either one of these philosophical paradigms holds all the answers for the church or that the gospel of Jesus Christ is entirely contained by either one. The church has been around through many philosophical paradigm shifts and will continue to live through many more, so we aren't going to try to convince you that we need to hold to one philosophical paradigm and get rid of the other to be faithful Christians.

The paradigm isn't the problem. The problem is that *young people are leaving the church*. That dynamic, we think, has a lot to do with the fact that young people are getting the impression that the paradigm of their faith has no place in the church and that a rift between the generations begins to emerge. Therefore, part of our purpose is to challenge the reader to reimagine his or her relationship with the church in light of this shift, not seeing the shift as an unredeemable rift but as an opportunity to give and receive hospitality.

In the first section of this book, we'll offer a brief sketch of some of the issues we've referred to in an attempt to illustrate some of the sociological, theological, and philosophical factors that have led to the placelessness of the young. There are many other books that explore the sociological shifts taking place, but our purpose is to offer some theological reflection on what makes the church unique and exploring what those sociological trends might mean for a body as distinctive as the church.

Keeping in mind the images of table fellowship and hospitality, the second section of the book engages particular stories of young people who have either left the church, found a place in the church, or find themselves struggling somewhere in between. We know that not every young person's struggle will be represented in its fullness, and not every theme related to the nature of the church will emerge in the stories of those in this book, but we've chosen to use particular stories and work from their particularity, reflecting theologically on them in ways that we hope offer a way forward for those who wonder if the church has a place for them. We also want each story to speak and to ask some important questions that move us toward postures of welcome and hospitality, opening places in the church for those who wonder if they presently have a seat at the table.

In the last section of the book, we will extrapolate further the themes that surfaced in the previous sections, exploring themes of hospitality, Trinitarian theology, particularity, and the kingdom of God, which will give us a theological foundation to suggest more than clever solutions and growth strategies but also ways of being Christ's disciples together, which will naturally open places for young people at the table and help the church to more faithfully be a sign and symbol of God's kingdom.

Hospitality is not what you pay for at a hotel or restaurant. The hospitality we're talking about is not for sale. This is hospitality that extends a genuine welcome to the stranger, the outcast, the other—an offer to pull up a chair and sit at the table and feast. It's something that many of us don't experience on a regular basis but something we think God is calling the church to be and a way that all people can find a place in the church.

In looking to Trinitarian theology and the associated ideas of particularity, we'll see that this particularity is an important and necessary aspect of authentic community, seen first in the divine community of the Father, Son, and Holy Spirit.

It's our deep desire that if you are encountering this book it will be for you a source of hope, whether you are a young person who wonders if there is a place in the church for someone like you or if you want to know if your own church can be the kind of body in which young people are welcome.

*Hope* is a tricky word, and the way we use it doesn't mean that we wish for a reality that will not be realized. Rather, hope is living inside the coming future that God has with a deep sense of trust that the one who promises is faithful. That's the kind of hope that can be transformative. May we together live in that hope, that God's hospitable presence will be at home in the church, extending welcome to those who are presently unable to find a place at the table. May our lives anticipate a full and overflowing banquet table where the outsider can enter in, be offered the genuine welcome of hospitality, and find a seat at the table.

# PART 1

# SETTING THE TABLE

# ASKING
# 1 FOR
# CRUMBS

**THE GOSPELS** are full of stories that rightly put us a bit on edge. Not the least of these is the story of Jesus and the Canaanite woman in Matthew 15.

A Canaanite woman from that vicinity came to him, crying out, "Lord, Son of David, have mercy on me! My daughter is demon-possessed and suffering terribly." Jesus did not answer a word. So his disciples came to him and urged him, "Send her away, for she keeps crying out after us." He answered, "I was sent only to the lost sheep of Israel."

The woman came and knelt before him. "Lord, help me!" she said. He replied, "It is not right to take the children's bread and toss it to the dogs." "Yes it is, Lord," she said. "Even the dogs eat the crumbs that fall from their master's table." Then Jesus said to her, "Woman, you have great faith! Your request is granted." And her daughter was healed at that moment *(Matthew 15:22-28)*.

Jewish men in Jesus' time were taught to pray, *Lord, I am grateful I was not born a Gentile, a woman—or a dog.* When this Gentile woman approached Jesus in front of a crowd of mostly Jewish men, you can imagine the embarrassment. Unflinching at her own disgrace, the woman cried out, "Lord, Son of David, have mercy on me! My daughter is demon-possessed and suffering terribly."

The disciples wanted her sent away. The woman wanted action. Jesus disappointed them both. He merely answered, "I was sent only to the lost sheep of Israel." The woman seemed to be outside the scope of the mission for the Jewish Messiah. But she also seemed not to care too much about that. After all, she had a suffering daughter. Who, for the love of a child, wouldn't go to the length of public humiliation for restoration? "Lord, help me!" she insisted.

We imagine Jesus' words carried quite a sting when he said, "It is not right to take the children's bread and toss it to the dogs." Dogs? That must have hurt.

Yet the woman did not seem fazed by the rhetorical bite. "Yes it is, Lord," she said. "Even the dogs eat the crumbs that fall from the master's table."

Then Jesus said to her, "Woman, you have great faith! Your request is granted." And her daughter was healed at that very moment.

On its face, this is the kind of story that would have moved the original readers of Matthew's Gospel. Matthew, after all, was writing specifically to a Jewish audience, making the case along Jewish lines that Jesus was the Messiah they had been waiting for. So Jewish readers would have understood how this woman wouldn't have had a place in the banquet the Messiah would come to host. The Messiah was coming to redeem Israel, not the other nations.

But something incredible happens in Matthew 15. The mission of the Messiah begins to surprise us, because it begins to expand in front of our eyes. Jesus' mission was so much bigger than any culture, ethnicity, or worldview. As He looked upon this woman, He didn't see someone who was naturally excluded from the banquet He was going to throw, a person who wouldn't have a place at the table. Instead, He saw her with the compassion of the Father and caught sight of "great faith" in a most unexpected soul. The wideness of the Kingdom Jesus had come to preach and practice drew this Gentile woman—the ultimate outsider—into the family of God.

It is also astounding to us that the Gentile woman did not see herself as deserving of anything. She understood the place of her rung on the social ladder. No true rebuttals were made, no passionate speech on the human rights theory of equality, no list of inner qualities and characteristics—not even an emotional plea for her worth in God's eyes. She acknowledged herself as a dog and merely asked for crumbs—the overflow of a meal to which she was not invited.

In response to this Gentile's humble request, Jesus commended her faith as "great," an honor given to only two people in all the gospel accounts—neither of whom were Jewish, but outsiders. Of course, you might still be put off at how our perfect, sinless Lord could call this desperate woman a dog. In the twenty-first century we cannot help but hear His words very differently than first-century Palestinians would have heard them, although that fact does little to settle the queasy feeling in our stomachs left by this passage.

THESE DAYS FEW CHRISTIANS QUESTION WHETHER THEIR ANCESTRAL HERITAGE OPENS A PLACE FOR THEM IN GOD'S PROMISED SALVATION.

Queasiness aside, the marvelous, salvific message in this passage is that Jesus affirmed her place in the kingdom of God. Her plight would no longer be outside the scope of God's redemptive work in creation. As far as any of the Jews of the day were concerned, the party was not for her, yet Jesus pulled up an extra chair to the table, for the banquet was about to begin.

These days few Christians question whether their ancestral heritage opens a place for them in God's promised salvation. We've read enough of Paul's letters (sometimes we've read them poorly, but we've read them all the same) to believe that Christ has expanded the scope of God's mission to the ends of the earth, every tongue, tribe, and nation. "There is neither Jew nor Greek, neither slave nor free, nor is there male or female, for you are all one in Christ Jesus," we read (Galatians 3:28). Still, there seems somehow to be more suspicion than ever regarding who is in and who is out of the promises of God.

In the 2008 United States presidential election, vice-presidential candidate Sarah Palin famously spoke about "real" America, describing it as more rural, conservative, and concerned with family values than the urbanized upbringing of her "community organizer" opponent. Comedians at *Saturday Night Live* latched onto Sarah Palin's description of "real" America. Tina Fey became a household name. The war of words was on as the right and left tried to coin more quick and catchy phrases to negatively describe each other. Sometimes it was just hilarious. Other times, it wasn't becoming of the way humans ought to speak about each other. Funny as it can sometimes be, our fear is that this same concept is being transplanted into our churches, the idea that there are *real* Christians, a category not defined by Christian creeds or biblical integrity but by particular culturally and philosophically defined worldviews. It may be that you've experienced this for yourself and that somewhere along the way others in the church have been a little suspicious of you.

The suspicion is especially strong along what seems to be largely generational lines. We have seen too many dear friends walk away from their churches, organized religion, and sometimes walk away from Christ completely because they so heavily felt the eye of suspicion. You can label the battle any way you like—emergent vs. traditional, modern vs. postmodern, missional vs. evangelical—the battle lines are largely age-related. Not that there is a magical age at which you become one or the other, but there is a major sociological shift between people who reached adulthood in the 1990s and 2000s from prior generations, especially concerning views on organized religion.[1] In one national survey, for example, sixty-one percent of young adults in their twenties who had been involved in the church as teenagers no longer identify with a worshiping body.[2]

IN ONE NATIONAL SURVEY, FOR EXAMPLE, SIXTY-ONE PERCENT OF YOUNG ADULTS IN THEIR TWENTIES WHO HAD BEEN INVOLVED IN THE CHURCH AS TEENAGERS NO LONGER IDENTIFY WITH A WORSHIPPING BODY.

So what's the problem? It's that this sociological shift leaves a generation displaced and begging for crumbs. It's not purposeful—not always, but it is happening. If you can stick with the metaphor, the church is the table, and there are plenty who have lost a seat at the table because they're on the wrong side of this sociological shift. There's a disconnect, and it's painful, not only to those who find they no longer have a seat at the table but also to the entire church, whether we realize it yet or not.

It's not that all young Christians have left the church. Of those who have stayed, some are content and doing their best to faithfully live out the gospel in their local congregations. If that's you, fantastic. We hope you find this book interesting and enlightening. But many others are struggling. Many are church-hopping or finding themselves sleeping in more Sunday mornings than not, even though they still identify with Christianity at some level. They're just looking for the right fit. Others are happy to find Christian connection through an assortment of religious services and traditions: attending their parents' church on Easter and Mother's Day, hooking up with a small group of young singles or couples affiliated with a nearby mega-church, and maybe hitting a random church with friends a few weekends a month. Others have found a church just recently, and they're even toying with the idea of committing to it, but it's pretty different from the faith tradition that raised them and introduced them to Jesus for the first time, and these people probably feel the loss of those roots, even while rejoicing in the sustenance their new church provides. Others are still attending the churches in which they grew up—or at least churches a lot like it—only to strain under the feelings of disconnection, confusion, frustration, suspicion, and maybe even placelessness.

We're assuming that if you're reading this book you've had some kind of experience and background with the church but that you may now be struggling to find a place within the church that taught you about faith in Jesus. You may feel as if your dreams and visions of what the church ought to be do not line up with the reality of your experience in the church, and that leaves you wondering if the church is the place for you. If that's you, we want you to know that as twenty-somethings we resonate with the angst and frustration that comes from wanting your church to be a little more like the kingdom of God you've been hearing about for so long. As people on the younger side of life, we, too, have had our share of questions, especially as we see a rift emerging between younger and older generations, and we wondered if the church is a place that really has space for our energy, passion, and faith.

But you may also be reading this book if you are a leader within the church who is discontent with the current trends affecting young people. If that's you, we want you to know how much we resonate with the heartbreak and frustration leaders experience who have poured years of their lives into discipleship for children and youth only to see them walk away. As pastors, we often struggle with the emotions of failure that come from doing everything we know how to do only to see young people turn away from the grace and mercy we long for them to receive.

Finally, we hope this book will serve to resource those who want to know more about this generational dynamic and what it might mean for both young and old Christians. You may, like many others in the church, be trying to be faithfully Christian and can't seem to understand why people are so entrenched in particular theological camps and using such fiery rhetoric and charging one another with being less than faithful, based upon paradigms and practices usually associated with particular age groups. If that's you, we hope this book will help bring you up to speed and calm some of the more significant fears about the leadership of the church being passed down to the next generation.

## SHOCK AND AFTERSHOCK

As Robert Putnam and David Campbell explain in *American Grace*, American religious life is experiencing the third seismic shock over the last half century.[3] The first—you guessed it—was the long 1960s, an era in which the civil religious institutions so fortified in the 1950s came under real scrutiny. No longer did people fill pews because of duty or a sense of pride and establishment. Instead, the country questioned many of the moral issues long dictated by a Judeo-Christian worldview (such as sex, drugs, and rock-n-roll). But by the time the late 1970s and early 1980s rolled around, an aftershock rolled out from the free love epicenter as large numbers of people who were deeply concerned with the tidal wave of moral and religious abandonment of the 1960s found their way to pews, especially in Evangelical churches.

In this second shock to the American religious landscape, the diversity of social and political opinions that once described American Christianity began to recede as "highly religious" people became more and more associated with conservatism. But the strong unity and social and political leverage the Christian right gained in the 1980s would ultimately become the setting of the stage for the third shock. Unfortunately, the third movement, as far as Campbell and Putnam can tell, involves a younger generation, those reaching adulthood in the 1990s and 2000s, the generation of the authors of this book, moving away from religious institutions.

The result of the third shock has been an increasing group called the *nones*, who claim no religious identity whatsoever. The *nones* tend to be college educated and raised in mildly religious households. Surprisingly, this increasing group isn't skeptical of faith. In fact, many consider themselves spiritual and religious; they even have a positive view of Jesus. But after experiencing the result of a somewhat oppressive Evangelical culture in the 1980s and 1990s, this younger generation has said, "If that's what religion is all about then it's not for me."[4]

> YOUNGER GENERATIONS ARE SEEKING TO EXPERIENCE THEIR FAITH IN WAYS THAT LOOK OR SOUND DIFFERENT FROM THEIR PARENTS.

In what Putnam and Campbell have illustrated, major shifts have taken place over the last two generations in American religious life. The subtext, then, is that those shifts have significant impacts in the lives of all generations. Because the younger generations have tended to turn away from the faith structures of their parents' and grandparents' generations, they are seeking to experience their faith in ways that look or sound different from their parents. Putnam and Campbell do not present to us a stark denial of faith in the younger generation but an aftershock of a major sociological shift out of which differences in the expression of faith arise. Those differences of expression often lead to confusion and possibly even suspicion between the generations, an idea we will explore more fully later.

Not long after Putnam and Campbell published their sociological findings in *American Grace*, *Christianity Today* published an article examining trends of young people leaving the church.[5] Drew Dyck, the author of the article, surveys several books that represent interviews with thousands of young adults and finds that most of the young people in North America had at some point in their lives been worshipers of Jesus. "Most unbelieving outsiders," he writes, "are old friends, yesterday's worshipers, children who once prayed to Jesus." Dyck goes on to write that he, like us, found incredible diversity in the stories young people tell about trying to find their place in the church. But again there is a common theme, says Dyck, in that most young people will attribute their exit of the church to something that happened *in* the church. It isn't so much that they have fundamental problems with the beliefs of the church as much as they have encountered something unwelcoming that left them wondering if they had a place there any longer. "Many de-conversions were precipitated by what happened inside rather than outside the church," Dyck writes. "Even those who adopted materialist worldviews or voguish spiritualities traced their departures back to what happened in church."

Part of what happens in the church to cause young people to question their place there is an emerging suspicion between the generations, Dyck points out. Perhaps this is the way it has always been. Perhaps older generations have always wondered why their children are so wieldy and impetuous. In what we've heard from young people, their placelessness is often associated with their church being confused by their kind of Christianity. They long to be faithful, they long to be disciples, and yet discipleship to Christ takes on different practices than their parents' generation, leaving some in the older generation confused and even a bit suspicious. That suspicion in turn leaves young people wondering if they still have a place in the church, if their practices of worship are a valid expression of their faith.

Young people have plenty of questions, too, and often they are asking questions that their parents did not have to wrestle with when they were young adults. This can lead to a sense of placelessness on the part of a young Christian struggling with either a different expression of Christian faith or the questions that accompany a growing and healthy faith.

"A generation of young Christians believes that the churches in which they were raised are not safe and hospitable places to express doubts," writes David Kinnaman.[6] There are certainly times when the questions of a young generation are just as perplexing to the church as their expressions of faith, sometimes leading to suspicion. In the face of such questions, it is important for the church to continue to offer hospitality to young people and to create space for them within the church to wrestle with doubt rather than cast their questions in terms that exclude them from the table.

As people who have come of age in the generations of the "nones," we are troubled that this kind of confusion and suspicion causes our generation to miss out on the incredible gift of God's redemptive salvation—but that the church, too, is missing out on the gift that is the presence of young people. We hear from those in our generation who are struggling to find a place in the church that they don't fit, often because of some kind of disproportionate attention being paid in the church to who is "in" and who is "out" at the banquet table.

To be clear, we are not relativists. We do not believe that the Christian faith is whatever you would have it be or a smorgasbord from which you can build your own spiritual "happy meal." And thanks be to God for this! If we are going to be redeemed, healed, and sanctified, it won't be a redemption, healing, or sanctification of our own invention. We have each spent years of training in theological studies so that we can be discerning servants when it comes to doctrine. However, we are also uneasy with the kind of religious life that is overtly concerned with who should not be invited to the table, because it's that kind of approach that young people tell us closes off their place at the banquet.

Jesus' action in the story of the Gentile woman is a better example of the kind of balance we would like to strike than anything we could come up with. As we've seen, the Gentile woman was a person who was definitely an outsider, a person who wasn't invited to the table. But as she came to Jesus with the faith that He could bring healing to her life and submitted herself to His instruction and mercy, she was welcomed by Jesus and given a place at the table.

The welcome of the Body of Christ is a wide welcome, a mercy-filled and gracious embrace, but it is predicated upon coming to Christ with the faith that His mercy will change our lives and make us different. The message of Christ's salvation is that you can come as you are but that you leave as a changed person, and that's great news. In other words, the church isn't just a big group of people who happen to get together in the general spirit of friendliness and feel good about who they are, but rather it is a particular and peculiar communion of those who have placed their faith in Christ, who have given themselves to His mission and mercy, who have been reconciled to one another by the Spirit. That's the kind of example in the world that can show how incredible God's grace is and reflect the glory for such an accomplishment to God.

And yet there are times when we church people bend a little bit to the temptation to set our own parameters, to write our own definitions, and to stand in the way of those who would come to Jesus in humility and submit to Him with the faith that He could transform their lives. We imperfect people, in other words, tend to be a little more anxious to define some as "insiders" and others as "outsiders" than Jesus does. As we've seen in Matthew 15, Jesus makes space for outsiders who come with "great faith," hoping for healing, wholeness, and redemption. A genuine welcome is preceded by a genuine faith.

We are finding that it is often young people who are seen as outsiders, as those who don't fit the mold of the faithful. Not that young people don't also fall to the temptation to define themselves as insiders and all others as outsiders, but when it comes to the church, they are a generation who wonders if their faith in Christ still qualifies them for a place at the table, especially when the outward expression of their faith looks so different from the outward expression of faith of their parents and grandparents. These expressions are those that sometimes confuse the church, and suspicion results. Could young people, like the Gentile woman, be offered a welcome by Jesus? Could they, based upon their faith in Christ's redemption, find that they, too, could be offered a place at the banquet?

We believe the answer is a hopeful and powerful *yes*. We think that God has given and continues to give the church what it needs to faithfully embody the kingdom of God, to welcome strangers and outsiders who come with great faith. It is with that hope that we offer this book to those who are wondering if they have a place any longer, those who wonder why their churches lack young people, those who remain present in their churches as a prophetic presence, and those whose particularity causes them to be viewed with suspicion.

Gladly we offer this in joyful hope, not that we can engineer a clever solution or begin to bang the church into an image that we think is fitting for an egalitarian, modern society, but that God continues to give the church what it needs to be the church. Sometimes those gifts are silent, strange, and surprising. May we have eyes to see, ears to hear, faith and humility enough to accept that God may be giving us what we need in the form of outsiders. Perhaps the gift of God can be seen in those who do not have a place at the table but whose ravenous hunger drives them to ask for nothing more than the crumbs that fall to the ground.

MAY WE HAVE EYES TO SEE, EARS TO HEAR, FAITH AND HUMILITY ENOUGH TO ACCEPT THAT GOD MAY BE GIVING US WHAT WE NEED IN THE FORM OF OUTSIDERS.

## BOLDLY ASKING FOR WELCOME

Consider the Gentile woman again. Even though the insiders of the day thought she didn't deserve an invitation to the party, she knew that there was only one table that could fill her hunger for wholeness. She would not be turned away. Boldly she asked for crumbs. She was content to sit at the feet of the guests like a dog and catch whatever might fall to the floor.

The image of a grown woman lapping the floor for crumbs is absurd. If you're revolted by the image, that's good: it's probably the point of using that particular image. But through her extended analogy she brought to light the reality of the hierarchy in which she was a victim, the reality of her placelessness. This is the kind of thing that we call "prophetic presence," an idea we'll unpack later in the book.

We doubt that she got up that morning intending to crusade for justice. After all, she had a little girl to care for. She just wanted wholeness and restoration, even if she had to be made the fool. But by the end of the story, Jesus lifted her up off the ground and gave her a seat at the table. The woman asked for crumbs and was welcomed as an honored guest in the kingdom of God.

The trouble is—we are rarely so bold. We think much of ourselves. We're not dogs. By the time we could understand full sentences, marketers were telling us that we had the power of selection and deserved to select, and we had the purchasing power to do so. We're taught that the only things that bring us the greatest fulfillment are those things that create an identity that gives us our desired status among our peers. And the message that comes through: our opinions matter; our voices ought to be heard. It's true that our voices, opinions, and particularities ought to have a place in the Kingdom, but with a caveat: so long as they come under the submission to Christ's Lordship. Oh, but there's a word that doesn't settle well: *submission*. We'll talk more about this later.

There are many who have been deeply scarred by the suspicion, word wars, or simple coldness of the generational collision we're outlining. Others merely sense a cooling in their own hearts and lives toward the church, the faith, the Savior. Healing begins in receiving God's good gifts. But moving from our wounds toward participating in God's gift-giving is no small thing. Finding a place in communities that have hurt us requires the rebuilding of trust, and reading a book won't rebuild that trust. But perhaps these next several chapters will provide space and time for our readers to enter into deep reflection about their place in the church.

# HOLD
2    THE
# RELIGION

WE HOPE that by encountering this book you will be encouraged to engage the church in a real and authentic way. We aren't going to pretend that the millennial generation is connecting with the church in the same way their parents have, because the sociological research tells a different story, as seen in the previous chapter.

Before we dive into the stories of some Christians who are struggling to find their place in the church, we thought that a few words to sketch our own story would be helpful in touching on some of the major themes of this book. It hasn't always been easy for us to find a place in the church, but in the various congregations we've been a part of over the last decade, we have been welcomed. Sometimes it's been easy for us to find a place, so part of our story will highlight the ways in which we were able to connect with the church. We also acknowledge that the church can unknowingly do things that might be challenging to young people, so we'll highlight those things and offer some brief reflections.

Every church we have served is a church we have loved dearly. Every church we have served has welcomed us. Our intention is to reflect a bit on our own experiences, the challenges of feeling at home in a new church and the ways in which we were able to find a place in the church. Our purpose in doing so is to offer a word of hope to those who wonder if they can be welcomed into the church, be it a large or small, mainline or Evangelical, urban or suburban congregation.

We'll also be honest about the parts of our journey in which we have witnessed the confusion and suspicion that emerges in the church along generational lines. We aren't particularly angry or disillusioned about that reality, but we do understand how it can contribute to young people wondering if the church has a place for them, which is why we'll go on to offer some reflections on the way those divisions did not have the final word in our finding a seat at the table.

In all honesty, we both love the church dearly. We're grateful for everything we've received from the church, and we're also incredibly hopeful that God is continuing to use the church to bring about the divine mission of healing and redemption in the world. We've seen too many good things take place in the church to think otherwise. Every church we've ever been a part of has been a community of imperfect but wonderful people whose lives have borne the marks of God's redemption. In fact, no church we've known has ever wanted young people to leave its fellowship. We can say without a doubt that every church we've worshiped with has taken active steps to reach out to our generation and has had a concern that there be a place for those who came of age in the height of roller blades, grunge music, and either one of the Bush administrations. That's probably what makes us wonder why young people have struggled so much to find a place in the church. If churches want young people to join them, where is the disconnect? We'll suggest a few points for consideration in this chapter, but with the understanding that the good people in each of our congregations have never actively sought to close themselves off or intentionally done anything to discourage young people from joining their communion.

In the spirit of full disclosure, we want young people to stay engaged in the church. We want to see their passions flourish and for the church to receive the gifts of an up-and-coming generation whose

EVERY CHURCH WE'VE EVER BEEN A PART OF HAS BEEN A COMMUNITY OF IMPERFECT BUT WONDERFUL PEOPLE WHOSE LIVES HAVE BORNE THE MARKS OF GOD'S REDEMPTION.

members are looking to give their lives to something bigger than themselves. And we're incredibly hopeful at a theological level, because we've seen that God has not abandoned the church and that the Holy Spirit is giving gift after gift in quiet, novel, and unexpected ways.

However, quiet and unexpected gifts are often not immediately seen as gifts. Sometimes we don't know how wonderful a gift is until long after it's been given to us. That's the sense we get with the way young people are engaging their faith in Christ. We get the sense that sometimes the church doesn't immediately recognize the gift it has received until long after it's been given. Our concern is that we as the church will have the eyes to see and the ears to hear what God is doing in the world and the way God is engaging a young generation in order to do it.

We were both born into church-going Christian families and have been attending church as long as we can remember. We both have at least one parent in ministry, and that usually comes with some long hours spent at the church for one reason or another. Our churches were both Evangelical, Protestant congregations, both affiliated with the Church of the Nazarene, and both gave us a lot that we are thankful for to this day.

When we went to college, we both knew we wanted to serve the church, and both of us had a distinct sense that God had called us to ministry and the years of study and preparation to that end. The church is one of those truly unique places in which you are literally required to love those with whom you work, and one of the best ways we knew to love our congregations was to devote ourselves to the long process of ministerial preparation and ordination.

We were told over and over again through college that it was time for us to make our faith our own, that our parents' faith wasn't going to be the faith that would sustain us, that we would need to come to a point of taking hold of our faith—or perhaps letting *it* take hold of *us*.

That's precisely what happened. Throughout our college years we found a church home in a place that was by all standards of numerical-based success unremarkable. Located in a troubled corner of San Diego, our church was a small community of believers who gathered every week around the profound promise of God's redemption. Our building wasn't flashy, our services were relatively long, and we didn't have much money to throw around, but the place was packed with young people. Many of them were college students from our campus across town, and many were students who had grown up in the neighborhood around the church, students who were supposed by the neighborhood to be statistics in the making. Gang violence, unemployment, drug abuse—it was all present, and according to the stats, more than half of the kids in that neighborhood would meet their demise by following one of those avenues toward destruction.

Nevertheless, week after week we gathered around the hope that Scripture promised and wrapped up every service standing around the common table of the Lord's Supper, singing about the hope we had for redemption because of the elements we held in our hands.

There was something significant about the hope of the gospel that was engaging to young people in our church. Each week we were challenged to live faithfully according to the hope of Christ's redemption. We were challenged to invest, to give of ourselves, and to make commitments beyond convenience. Those commitments often took the form of using whatever gifts we had to give. Students who had a talent in one area were given room to let that talent flourish. Granted, we needed the gifts of young people to sustain the ministry we had in place and sometimes depended entirely upon it for some ministries to continue functioning, but the church's ability to provide an outlet for whatever the young people had to bring was remarkable. Sometimes it resulted in Britney Spears cover songs as an offertory or less-than-perfect sermons delivered by college students, but it was always a place where young people found a seat at the table.

It was there that we were challenged to make a commitment to Christ and His Church and also given the room to sit alongside those who were much older and be heard. Our ideas weren't always wonderful, but we were heard nonetheless. It was the combination of the call to commitment to God's redemptive mission, along with the space to exercise that commitment that we experienced in those days, that has a lot to do with why we are still so passionate about serving the church today.

After we were married, it came time to take the difficult step of leaving everyone we knew and our comfortable southern California lifestyle and let our faith take hold of our lives. We moved to Kansas City, began seminary, and connected with a local congregation of about one hundred fifty salt-of-the-earth people who loved being the church together. Both our seminary and our church were affiliated with the denomination we had known since we were children, so at some level we felt glad that we were at home.

AS WE BEGAN TO DIG
MORE DEEPLY INTO OUR
THEOLOGICAL STUDIES,
WE ALSO BEGAN TO
QUESTION CERTAIN
ASPECTS OF OUR OWN
TRADITION'S WAY OF
DOING THINGS.

But like being at home with family, there are always those things that are a bit strange at times. As we began to dig more deeply into our theological studies, we also began to question certain aspects of our own tradition's way of doing things. Why did we do such a good job of loving Jesus but have such a difficult time translating that love into social action? If our denominational tradition started with working with the poor in the inner cities of the United States, why did it seem that so many of our churches had moved out of the city and into the suburbs? Why had our memories become so short that the people at church could talk about urban issues only in terms of "bad neighborhoods"?

Why did we tend to think of living a holy life in only legalistic terms? Why did we claim to be part of a larger Christian communion but were so suspicious of other traditions and denominations? Why did everything have to be so structured and institutionalized? If we were supposed to be the people of God, why did we seem to fight with each other about the most ridiculous things possible? Why was there such a lack of emphasis on preparing pastors well and a near pride in avoiding seminary training?

Like teenagers coming to their own sense of identity within their family, we began to wonder more and more about why our strange relatives went about being the family in the awkward ways that they did. We still loved them, of course, but they could really be frustrating to us at times. We never stopped seeing the incredible potential of our churches, and we never stopped hoping that God was truly using our churches for divine purposes. In fact, we longed to see that become a reality. There were times of desperate prayer that God would heal the church where it was wounded and let it be used for God's redemptive mission. But there were also times when it seemed that our churches would have been just as satisfied with appearing to engage in redemptive purposes while actually making the color of the carpet, the sound of the music, or the style of worship a top priority. Even for people who deeply love the church they are committed to serving, that can be incredibly frustrating. We wanted to engage, we wanted to do lots of things, but it seemed as if our church family had a different set of concerns, different outlooks, different levels of interest.

All in all, we sometimes felt as if there wasn't much of a place for us. We had big dreams, and we wanted to see the church engage a broken world, but that often meant that the church would need to change in some respect. And change never comes easy.

Like so many people our age, we were restless and energetic, working long hours to pay the bills so that we could pay for our education and make an impact. We were eager and probably a bit impetuous, wanting to move quickly to engage a world around us in whatever ways we could. The question, however, is whether or not we could find a place in the church with all of our desire to change things and move quickly. Was there room for us and all our passion? Did we have a seat at the table?

As we reflect on our journey, we have come to understand that, yes, there is a place for us at the table and, yes, there is a place for us in the church, with all our desire and energy. But there were also lots of other places that were open to our energy in ways that the church was not. There were entire service organizations who depend upon young energy to do their work, job managers who were looking for young talent at a cheap wage, hip up-and-coming churches across town who had lots of young people engaged in creative ministry. All these places seemed to be going out of their way to make space for our passions, to give us room to try new things (and fail, if necessary), to pull out a chair and give us a seat at the table.

In the stories we've heard through researching for this book, a theme began to emerge that was also present in our own journey, suggesting that young people didn't seem to fit in the established church. There were lots of other places where their youthful vitality and idealism were seen as an asset, while the established church tended to view it as a liability. So we began to wonder why this was such a common theme with the young people we talked to.

Why did our churches always talk about ways of welcoming young people while the young people didn't feel as if their passion was as welcome in the church as it was in the other places? In something we saw as a sad trend, young people began taking their energy elsewhere, sensing that the church wasn't the place where they could truly engage a broken and hurting world.

Could part of this be the youthful angst of the YouTube generation simply being youthful and not working from a broader historical perspective? Yes, we think that's definitely possible. But theologically, we also began to wonder if we as the church were not seeing what God was giving in terms of the gifts that young idealists had to offer. And we also began to take seriously the frustrations that we heard young people articulating, wondering why their passion and energy were welcomed in so many other places. Were we missing out on a gift being given to the church and the world by God?

We took these stories and began placing them alongside our experience in the church. Nothing about our experience in the church suggested that the church was looking for ways to turn young people away. In fact, there was often much discussion in the various churches we've been part of as to how we could engage and welcome the twenty-something and thirty-something crowd. And when we began to take these desires and compare them to what we were hearing from young people, we wondered why there seemed to be such a disconnect.

The church wanted young people, young people wanted to engage in God's mission of redemption, so what was the problem? In our own story and in the stories of others, we began to sense that there was a generational disconnect, born not of ill intent but out of confusion that sometimes was accompanied by some amount of suspicion. That suspicion, we saw, would signal to young people that there just wasn't really room for their passion and their desire to move and change and engage. It was never intentional, of course. In none of our churches had we ever experienced people who wanted to actively turn away young people or cease to join in God's mission of redemption. But there was often confusion between the generations. While one generation saw engagement in God's mission as one set of ministries and experiences, another generation saw it differently. And that's where the confusion tended to enter the situation, along with some amount of suspicion— and ultimately an unestablished group of energetic twenty-somethings looking for another place to invest their passion.

Shortly after moving to Kansas City and beginning our seminary studies, Shawna noticed that there was an age gap in the ministry at our church, so she asked about starting a gathering for people who had graduated from college who weren't sure if they were ready to join the adult Sunday school class as their primary association on a Sunday morning. Because having young people is something it seems every church wants, it wasn't hard to gain permission to get a Sunday class for millennials up and running. There was a room open at the time, but the classroom style of the space didn't seem to be a very hospitable space for a gathering of friends to discuss life and Scripture together, so we moved the gathering around the corner to the local coffee shop. Besides, we loved the idea of being present in the community, of being visible outside of the walls of the church, and having the opportunity to touch the neighborhood at least once a week. The first few months were slow. Three or four of us gathered, caught up on life, read Scripture together, and reflected on it.

Before long our small group began to grow, and our time together began to take on a character of truthful and significant discussion. We opened Scripture, we let it speak, we disagreed with one another about its meaning, and it was fantastic. The group was pretty eclectic as well. What had been originally intended as a place for young college grads to gather, became a welcome place for parents, both single and married, a few folks who were planning their retirement, those who were enrolled in college, those on both sides of the law—both offenders and enforcement.

Gathering around Scripture compelled us to begin seeking ways to serve and engage our community through our local rescue mission and our neighborhood organizations, something that happened just about as many times as our game nights in each other's homes outside of church. At the risk of sounding a bit dramatic, there was something to the group that reminded us of the roots of our church's history of groups of Christians opening Scripture, praying together, and serving together. The group was certainly far from perfect, but it was just different enough that it seemed to us, at least, that we saw signs of the kingdom of God every time we came together. And if we're honest, we have to admit that we liked that it was a bit chaotic, that our little group didn't have a clever title, that it was pretty organic every time we met together.

While we were meeting at the coffee shop, the church was happy to bless our group. If we happened to attract more young people to the church, great, but if we didn't, at least we were buying our own pastries and weren't taking up a room that could be used for other purposes. But eventually it was hard to hear one another at the coffee shop over the noise of the bean grinder and the milk steamer. The group just didn't fit in the coffee shop anymore.

The church was quick in its response. Genuinely excited that a group of young people was gathering and that the ministry was growing, the congregation did everything it knew to do to set the group up for success. A room was opened for the group (now decorated with beautiful and engaging decor), the official Sunday school rolls were amended to account for a new class, and we were greeted with open arms when we walked through the doors for our first gathering. The encounter was, to us, incredibly fascinating.

In the last chapter we touched on the idea of confusion and suspicion that sometimes characterizes the generational divide. We want to be clear in saying that this divide, wherever we've encountered it in the church, has never been anything other than well-intentioned. In fact, it usually has its roots in the purest of intentions that one could imagine. Such was our experience. When our church saw a group of young people forming and growing, the congregation did everything it knew to do to bless the group and set it up for success. For their generation, that meant organizing, selecting a name, selecting a teacher, ordering curriculum, arranging a classroom, and inviting their friends. But as we've touched on in the last chapter, that just isn't the way a millennial generation tends to express their faith, and thus, that possibly leaves both generations a bit confused in situations such as ours.

"What is the name of your class?" the church wanted to know. "What curriculum will you be using? Will you take up a collection for donuts and coffee?" While we tend to think that being organized is a good thing and hasn't really hurt much, there was also a sense that our group didn't really fit into the structures and systems that we were being asked to fit into. Naming ourselves seemed foreign and inorganic. Curriculum seemed stifling to what was actually taking place in our gatherings. The kind of ministry we wanted to do wasn't a typical "Sunday School" thing, so when we tried to do a strange kind of ministry under a Sunday School system, confusion was the result. And sometimes confusion is accompanied by suspicion, and suspicion is accompanied by conflict, and conflict is accompanied by pain.

Obviously, no one wanted to see a group of people in the church hurt. We are incredibly thankful for a church that would give of itself to make space for a group of misfit young people to gather around Scripture and prayer and discussion about what this all means to live faithfully in the world. But our experience was also one fairly similar to ones that we hear many young people talking about. We hear stories that the church wasn't entirely sure what to do with them, their strangeness, their passions, their music, their politics, their questions, their hopes, their desire for change. With all good intention, the church is excited to have young people but isn't sure how to pull out a chair at the table and make them feel welcome. Sometimes the church is thrilled to have young people as long as the young people function a lot like the older generation. After all, the older generation has this church thing down. They're good at it. More of them are in church on a given Sunday than those of the millennial generation, so if anyone knows how to do things for the church, it would be the older generation, right? This, we think, is when confusion begins to enter, when young people begin to wonder if there is a place for them in the church because they tend to express their faith so differently.

While we've seen many churches who are excited to have young people but often with the condition that the young people look a whole lot like the older people and get excited by the same structures, programs, ministries, music and worship style, we have also seen the suspicion work the other way, that the younger generation is suspicious of the older generation, mainly because they're confused by the older generation's ways of going about ministry.

When the time came to pursue further education, it required us to leave the church we had grown to love and find a home in a new congregation hundreds of miles away. On the outskirts of Chicago, we were welcomed into a historic mainline church that was even more "established" with its beautiful brick-and-column buildings on a well-kept campus at the heart of town. For the first two months of our time there, we didn't see anyone else at church within fifteen years of our age. It didn't seem to make much sense. Our neighborhood was brimming with young professionals, children in tow, and there were thriving college communities bordering our town on either side. So why weren't there young people in our church?

OUR NEIGHBORHOOD WAS BRIMMING WITH YOUNG PROFESSIONALS, CHILDREN IN TOW, AND THERE WERE THRIVING COLLEGE COMMUNITIES BORDERING OUR TOWN ON EITHER SIDE. SO WHY WEREN'T THERE YOUNG PEOPLE IN OUR CHURCH?

When Haley came to our church for the first time, it was a banner occasion. She was a recent grad from college, married with a baby on the way. It was everything our church had hoped to see. And so in their excitement, several people in the church began to introduce her to the rest of the congregation. "We'd like you to meet Haley, a potential member," said a dear saint of the church with an excited twinkle in his eye. But there was something about being introduced to another human being as a "potential member" that made us wince. By the expression on her face, it didn't feel right to her either.

Was there anything wrong with being introduced that way? Maybe. Maybe not. But it began to tell us a bit more about the underlying currents that seemed to carry young people into the church, only to wash them out after a few weeks.

As we began to reflect on what we had seen take place, we saw some of the most saintly people in our church do exactly what they would have wanted for themselves when they were Haley's age. For them, church membership was a given. It's simply a matter of selecting the church you will join, and then you begin the organized process of becoming a member. But for Haley and for many of the other young people we have seen come through the doors of the church, they aren't looking for membership in an organization. They are often looking for significant, meaningful connection, a profound engagement in something real, something that could be described only as God-sized redemption.

Psychologist Jeffrey Jensen Arnett's research on young adults showed that "Emerging adults tend to personalize their relationship with God in a way that makes participating in organized religion unnecessary or even an impediment to the expression of their beliefs."[1] While young adults are certainly open to belief in God, according to Arnett's findings, they are nowhere near as prone to associate that belief with membership in an institution.

To highlight one aspect of this sociological shift at work, it is the association with institutional structure itself that seems to be the barrier to many young people, while association with organized institutions tends to be more of a hallmark of the "builder" generation. In what we've experienced, a generation that readily connects its faith to the experience of an institutional organization with presidents, committees, and clubs wonders why young people won't come to faith in the same way. In our church near Chicago we often heard the older generation remark, "Why won't young people come to our church? We're a good church, aren't we?"

There was confusion in their voices, because they really have some of the most well-organized and involved committees and clubs in town. This is how they came to the church as young people, and they wonder why the current generation of twenty-somethings isn't having the same experience. Their generation is also the age of the rise of social organizations such as the Elks Lodge or the Rotary Club, which also attract a mainly older generation. It was the strong structure, organization, and committee-based institutions that attracted them.

But as culture changes, young people are less likely to connect to church in the same way. Rather than understanding themselves as members of established organizations, they are far more interested in engaging something that will be organically, rather than structurally, significant and faith-challenging. It's deep challenge and discipleship, rather than membership, that seems to spark their imaginations.

Can deep challenge and discipleship take place through the committees and organizations? We think so, and we see it happening all the time. Yet the generation that wonders if there is a place for this is a younger generation that has been formed to associate less structurally, and they often wonder if there's anything for them if they aren't comfortable signing up for a club or committee.

Another couple arrived at church shortly after we met Haley. They were established and professional but younger than a majority of the congregation. When we talked to them for the first time, they told us they had been looking for a church to join and that this church was going to be the place. Inside of two weeks, they had been assigned to various committees and began serving faithfully and effectively.

The church was elated. This is *exactly* what they wanted to see happening. They wanted to see young people show up, ready to serve the already-existing structures. We have to say that we were incredibly impressed by the couple as well. They were amazing and added a lot to the church. "That's what we need," one of the members of the congregation mentioned to Tim. "We need more couples like them!"

The problem we both saw, however, was that most young couples aren't looking to show up and serve on committees. They don't show up asking for membership papers. They show up looking for something beyond themselves, deeper than anything they can find in the bar scene or sports league. For better or for worse, this is simply what we're hearing from young people. They aren't looking for organized activities as much as they are looking for something authentically divine. Rather than signing up for a club to find relationships, the young people we hear from are more prone to joining those with whom they have already formed relationships at whatever clubs or organizations they happen to be a part of.

Many times, if it's a social club or a softball team, there are other places that can do that better than the church. But the church is that unique body that gathers under the name of Christ, assembled by the Spirit to the glory of the Father. And that was another point of disconnection we sensed: if the church was primarily a membership-based social organization, the gospel of Christ and the redemptive mission of God can easily become a secondary category. We don't think that it's a purposeful shift, but it is a shift that we have sensed nonetheless and one we think has become a factor in many young people sensing that the church isn't a place for them, especially if they are looking for something authentic to what the church is. In other words, if the church is primarily a social organization without a strong theological identity, it seems to be fundamentally uninteresting to those searching for a community that will engage their passions and enliven their imaginations.

In our journey, the congregations that have been able to retain youth are those that have been the most forward about identifying with their Christian theological tradition. In what we are hearing from young people who want to plug in to the church, taking theological identity seriously is nothing that is driving young people away from the church, but rather the opposite is in effect. In what seems to be a paradox, the churches who ask the most of their young members and who connect their ministry as closely as possible with Christian identity are those that are able to retain youth.

In October 2006 *Time* published an article that marveled at the strange trends of youth groups that had adopted theologically substantive ministry models and their ability to retain youth and engage their faith. "Believing that a message wrapped in pop-culture packaging was the way to attract teens to their flocks, pastors watered down the religious content and boosted the entertainment," explains Sonja Steptoe-Bellflower, the article's author. "But in recent years churches have begun offering their young people a style of religious instruction grounded in Bible study and teachings about the doctrines of their denomination." Those young people who were most engaged, the article goes on to highlight, were those who were given opportunities for engagement, for ministry and service in the church, all within the framework of theological intentionality.

A common theme in the stories we have heard from those who have been able to find a place in the church is that their communities of faith have been able to capture their imagination in ways that have connected an unabashed theological identity with the passions of young people. Those students who have remained in the church have communicated to us that they stayed with the church not really because they made an overtly conscious decision to join an organization but because somewhere along the way a connection was made between their passions and the redemptive mission of God in the world. Mere social connection rarely captures the imaginations of those who are looking for a way to meaningfully engage their context.

Soon after arriving at our church near Chicago, Shawna, who was the director of the youth ministry, hosted a gathering of all the parents so they could get to know the new youth pastor and see what her ministry would be like. She laid out her ideas, her vision for the ministry, and the approach she was planning to take the students through the story of John's Gospel. After she had offered her hopes for the upcoming year in the new ministry, one of the parents remarked, "This seems awfully—religious. I thought this was a place for students to get together and hang out." We quickly learned that "religious" was not a favorable descriptor of ministry and that some in the church actually saw it as a liability. In raising this concern, the parent simply wanted to be sure the group would thrive and grow, that students would be attracted to the church and not driven away by being offered the stale husk of religion. The exchange, it seemed to us, was a significant indicator as to why the church seemed to lack young people.

What researchers Christian Smith and Melinda Lindquist Duncan have uncovered, however, is that the young people whose imaginations have been captured are those who associate with churches that challenge them to engage deeply in the tradition of their faith. Smith and Duncan "observe a clear empirical fact that comports with theoretical and theological expectations: strengthening the faith lives of youth does, and so should, involve the formation of religious practices."[3]

In our view, young people can generally find surface-level fun anywhere, and when all the possibilities for that kind of fun are compared, the church usually isn't the flashiest. In other words, if it's only surface-level fun young people are searching for, hundreds of other places stand ready to outpace the church. But when we talk to young people who are seeking a place in the church, they want something far more than surface-level fun, and those who have found a place in the church are those who were challenged by their faith communities to identify with their tradition through practices of prayer, reading Scripture, and church attendance. Social interaction with others is certainly not to be dismissed, but if it is to capture their imagination, that social interaction must ask something more of young people, and it must be rooted in something larger than fun for fun's sake.

This, we think, isn't discouraging but incredibly hopeful, precisely because the church is that completely unique body that assembles around something deeper, more powerful, and far more interesting than what's found in dance clubs and sports leagues. The church is that place in which the redemptive hope of Christ's gospel is proclaimed, heard, and realized, where joy beyond mere happiness is present and where people find that deep commitment to Christ's gospel is a bondage that results in incredible, mind-boggling freedom.

The temptation to shy away from significant identification with Christ's gospel has resulted in a brand of faith that Smith and Duncan have termed "Moralistic Therapeutic Deism."[4] In this kind of religious experience, God is a distant creator who requires little but stands ready to bless those who are generally "good people," nice, happy, and polite. Religious expression in this vein requires little and gives a lot, mainly with the goal of making you feel as good as possible about who you are but rarely suggesting that faith in Christ will change you in some way, because you don't need to change the good person you already are. As Drew Dyck has written, when this is what the church offers to young people and it "crashes on the hard rocks of reality, we shouldn't be surprised to see people of any age walk away."[5]

Along our journey, our congregations in San Diego and Kansas City were really strong in the area of gospel-centric life and proclamation. Young people were constantly called to something beyond themselves, and it inspired their imaginations. But it's been our experience that when the call to submit to something beyond ourselves fades, so does a young person's interest in that community. Why, goes the logic, should I give my life to something that is only surface-deep? It's our hope that those who are seeking a place in the church would be challenged at every level not only to give themselves to God's mission of redeeming the world through the good news of Christ but also to be prophetically present in their churches, reminding their congregations that we assemble under the promise of Christ's salvation rather than the anticipation of a "nice experience" at church each week that leaves us unchanged.

Is any of this reason to despair, to simply stop trying? Not at all. Again, we continue to be in awe of the way in which God continues to give gifts through the presence of the millennial generation. But what about those who are struggling to find a place in the church? What about those who are encountering a kind of confusion about their longing to see the church faithfully live God's mission of redemption and healing? What options are left? We suppose this is a question we have wrestled with throughout our journey as well. Why stick with the church? Why not find places where we aren't met with confusion or even suspicion? Why not engage our passion and energy elsewhere?

We can't necessarily prescribe a one-size-fits-all answer, but we do know that any answer we can offer to those questions must begin with a hopeful anticipation and grateful realization of the way God continues to use the church for the sake of the world's healing. In other words, we can't really offer a lot of hope for those who are struggling to find a place in the church without first pointing to the real hope that we believe is present in the church. If the church were not what God is actually doing in the world right now, it would be easy to walk away. But the church *is* what God is actually doing in the world, even in spite of wrinkles and problems. And because of this reality, we can see hope for those who are wondering if the church still has a place for them and if their passions and desires have a place in the communion of the church.

**GOD CONTINUES TO SURPRISE US, TO GIVE UNEXPECTED MEANS THROUGH WHICH WE ARE REDEEMED AND HEALED.**

We're going to go a bit more in-depth into these ideas later, but very briefly, we find incredible hope in God's long history of redeeming the world in new and unexpected ways and that young people may be a means of God's surprising activity, and we can't get away from that. We see the way our generation isn't nearly as apathetic as is often reported and how a deep desire on their part is often translated into desires to engage the world in sustainable, profound, and global ways. God has a way of working out the world's salvation in strange and unexpected ways. Jesus himself, after all, was probably the most surprising way of all.

One way of telling the Christian story is that God chose to work in a way so strange, so unexpected, so unorthodox that many simply couldn't believe it. The same instinct, we think, is still alive. God continues to surprise us, to give unexpected means through which we are redeemed and healed, but because they are so unexpected, we often have trouble seeing them or believing that God would do such a thing. It's our prayer that we would be faithful enough to see the surprising ways God is redeeming the world and humble enough to accept God's new ways of redeeming.

If we take these two things side by side (God still uses the church, and God acts in surprising ways), there is a sense in which we long for the church to remember both that God enlists it in the mission of redemption and that this redeeming work can appear in strange, new ways, such as through the presence of young, passionate, talented, impetuous, gifted, questioning, and faithful people. In other words, we want to maintain a kind of prophetic presence in the church, to remind the church that it is so much more than a mere social club, and that when the church turns its back on the strange way God calls young people into the divine mission of redemption, the church is missing out on an opportunity to join in the most joyous experience one could know: the joy of God's healing, redemption, and salvation. A prophetic presence stands as a reminder to the church to look for God's surprising ways of redeeming the world and to open itself to these novel movements of His Spirit. These movements are consistent with God's long history of saving the world but may, in fact, be unobvious and difficult to discern.

We desperately want eyes to see and ears to hear what God is doing and to join in that redemptive work, and we want the church to remain open to seeing and hearing His startling and unanticipated ways of redeeming the world.

# PART 2

# TELLING THE STORIES

# IS THIS
## 3  A
# FAKE ID?

AS A CHILD, Lynn's identity was wrapped up in her church. She was the pastor's kid. Everyone knew her, and she knew everyone. Her father's position gave her the inside scoop into what happened and why, who was who, and what made each person tick. Roger was the guy who fixed cars. Heidi was a talented artist. Dennis did roofing. She knew who every person was and how his or her unique gifts were woven into the fabric of the church.

It may not have been explicitly said to her, but Lynn understood that you patronize the businesses of people in the congregation. Today she might refer to that as Christian solidarity, but she didn't have that language back then. That was just the way her family life operated—intricately connected to the life of the church and the people who made up that distinctive community.

As Lynn matured into high school, the signs of the church continued to be written all over her life. Sunday School, youth group, camp, retreats—she was always there. On Sunday mornings if Lynn wasn't involved on the worship team, that week she could probably be found running the slides (remember those?) for the overhead projector. The only Sundays Lynn wasn't in church were on the few-and-far-between vacation weeks.

Even though it was an expectation of Lynn's parents and congregation that she and her siblings be a part of everything the church did, as Lynn recalls, they all truly loved it. Never did a Wednesday night come around when Dad had to give the stern talk about the discipline of church life and importance of participation to shame them into the station wagon to be dropped off at youth group. Participation in the church was such a deep part of Lynn and her siblings that they went about it all with a real enthusiasm.

When Lynn went off to college, she realized for the first time in her life that she didn't *have* to go to church. Although she had never really been forced to go in the past, this new sense of freedom from expectations carried with it a certain excitement. No one was counting on her to run the slides. She wasn't obligated to help with mid-week activities. There was no one waiting for her to show up Sunday morning.

So she didn't.

Several months passed, and Lynn didn't bother getting out of bed on Sunday mornings. The beach was there, time with friends, just about anything other than submitting to some kind of obligation to go find a place to worship. As fall gave way to winter that year, Lynn began to realize that she was missing something. When she was really honest with us, she revealed that it wasn't her dad's deep theological sermons she missed, or being together with the people in the church, or an encounter with the Holy Spirit in a worship service.

She missed playing music.

Although she was a talented musician, Lynn went to college to study writing and literature rather than music theory and performance. She missed playing with a church worship team, practicing the songs for the week, arranging worship sets that had a nice flow yet having the freedom to improvise and experiment with other capable musicians. So she connected with a Sunday night worship service a local church was starting on her college campus. It was a brand-new service the church was trying to launch, and they needed, well, everything—including musicians. Lynn was in.

A couple of years later, the pastor in charge of the service left. Because it was a service for college students, the sponsoring church placed a lot of trust in the student leadership and gave them an incredible amount of space and patience. They were free to try new things, to learn, to fail, to try again. And the students loved it. The trust and freedom gave them a feeling of ownership that drove those students to a real depth of commitment to the service and one another. Whether it was setting up prayer stations, draping fabric, or preparing the communion elements every week, these students came through. Lynn believes that lots of churches say they want to see a ministry in which young people have ownership and display this kind of commitment, but few churches are really prepared to give them the kind of trust and freedom that allowed this service to blossom.

It didn't take long before the service became much more than a place to play music. Lynn had become fully invested. The community that gathered on Sunday nights now had a claim on her life and made a deep mark on her identity. The room where they met was a sacred space. Lynn laughed when remembering that they used to play a relaxation CD someone picked up at Target while their little congregation gathered. While she recognizes that there is nothing holy about that CD, it became so closely associated with her encounters with Christ in those services that still today she can go into a Target and hear that CD and suddenly be transported back to those services and that sacred space.

After Lynn graduated from college, the service that had come to be a place of identity formation for her went through a leadership transition and was soon cancelled. Lynn got a job in the city and decided to make her college town home—for a little while at least. It seemed to make sense that she also find a home in the same church that had sponsored the Sunday night service that had been a place of such grace and growth, especially as she made the transition from being a college student to a young working adult of sorts.

For the first time since she had lived with her parents, Lynn began plugging into a church with people of all ages. Because of the church's proximity to a college campus, there were many students in the congregation, but other church members seemed to expect the students to come and go every August and May without ever really changing the true makeup of the church. Lynn wasn't one of those students anymore, despite the fact that she was frequently asked about her major during the greeting time of the worship service.

In the meantime, Lynn's job in the city began to open new opportunities for her, and she started developing a name and identity in the community. Her job fulfilled everything she had dreamed of during those late nights working on college classwork. Her work allowed her to work with other interesting writers and develop great relationships with coworkers who were really different from the friends she had grown up with as a pastor's kid in a small town. If any of her coworkers had grown up in religious homes, none of them really practiced any kind of faith in adulthood. In her business, any connection to faith organizations can be a real detriment to one's reputation. Lynn recounted stories of people in her field who had been discredited because they were affiliated with churches or organizations that were branded as religiously bias to their colleagues.

Lynn, who by this time was on the worship team for her new church, became acutely aware of the image this church might give to outsiders. Could this church be the next one caught in a media scandal about bigotry, sex, finances, or the scandal *de jure*? Did the identity of this congregation line up with her identity as an intellectual? Standing on the platform week after week with the rest of the musicians, she was assumed to be some kind of leader in the congregation. But how might the views, practices, or people in this church reflect on her work? Could her association in this congregation scar her reputation outside of it? As the questions lingered, her very identity came into play.

After a few years of living with a growing sense of anxiety about her work and church association, Lynn stepped down from the worship team. She still loved playing music in the church, but she recognized that she was entering a new season of life and was struggling to adjust her practices accordingly. Once she was no longer a member of the worship team, Lynn realized just how little people in the church authentically knew her. Outside of her role as a musician, there was confusion about who she was, something she realized as she continued to answer questions about what she was studying in college four years after she had graduated. She was really known only by this one thing she had to offer to the church—she was the girl who played in the worship band.

As a single woman in her mid-twenties, Lynn found it hard to fit into any of the groups of that church. She felt as if it were assumed she wouldn't want to join gatherings of young couples. And though her church didn't make a big deal of it, she feared the kind of "single mingles" activities churches often have. Her age and marital status didn't occur to her to be the most important aspect of her identity that would then guide her association in the church. A group of writers, she thought, would be the group she would relate to, no matter what their ages. Maybe then, she thought, her church would know her in the same deep way her parents knew Dennis the roofer and Heidi the artist.

Perhaps it was the need to politely explain yet again to a member of the congregation that she didn't have a major but had actually graduated nearly a half-decade earlier that broke the proverbial camel's back.

Whatever it was, Lynn came to a place in her life where she wasn't sure she had a place in the church anymore and decided to take a break from her congregation. "I wouldn't say I walked away from the church entirely, but I definitely wasn't going." Did she have some serious doubts about her faith? Sure. But she still identified as a Christian and still had a love for Christ and Christ's people. She simply wanted some space from the people in the church.

> LYNN CAME TO A PLACE IN HER LIFE WHERE SHE WASN'T SURE SHE HAD A PLACE IN THE CHURCH ANYMORE AND DECIDED TO TAKE A BREAK FROM HER CONGREGATION.

Lynn was no longer the girl who played on the worship team. Once again, there was no one expecting her to show up on Sunday mornings or counting on her assistance with the operations of church life. For one year, Lynn kept her distance from the church. Much like her early college days, she was once again experiencing a kind of freedom. But once again that freedom didn't feel too freeing, because once again she was missing something. This time it was something more than a place to play music.

When Lynn told us her story, she was just returning to the church after her year-long hiatus. She still doesn't play music for the church and says it may take quite a while before she is ready to be that public with her participation. She says she doesn't know how to fix the things that were "freaking me out" before and still feels the need to nuance an answer when someone in the community asks about her church. But for Lynn, "There is something about what church is, this particular community and the weekly meeting of that assembly and the chance to find myself in it that is drawing me back." She says she is still not entirely sure why she fits there or how she fits there. Still, the communal remembrance and routine of the weekly gathering helps her better understand who she is and how God created her.

Lynn is hoping to find something more in the church than simply filling a role in the band or the adult singles group. It's easier for groups such as churches to just place people into simple societal categories, because it seems too difficult to actually carry with us the many stories that make up the many different people in that group, she told us. If Lynn is going to truly find her identity in Christ, she will need a church that welcomes the roundness of her story and the particularity of her identity in non-generic and particular ways, in ways that invite her to really know and be known by God.

Lynn's story has helped us consider the question of identity when young people come to a place where they no longer feel they have a place in the church. Her story has highlighted for us what happens when the particular identity of a young person is homogenized into the group of "young people" who must all want the same kind of age-based identification in the church.

But when we hear Lynn's story, we hear that there is a kind of searching that is going on for identity beyond age classification or interest groups. We also hear a challenging concept that we would like to use this chapter to unpack a bit, a concept that maintains the particularity of identity in the church while at the very same time asks that our identity be found first in God's story.

## STORIED PEOPLE/PEOPLE OF THE STORY

This last year we put an entire series of documentaries about the Kennedy family on our Netflix queue. Now here is a family that might cause us to think, *Haven't there been entirely enough books written and movies made about these people? Don't we know everything there is to know about them?* Yet we devoured the series, so interested with even the tiniest new revelation, because with every story, every document, every conversation and encounter we get a slightly different picture of the people involved.

We are "storied" people. Our lives unfold as a series of stories, each one formed by the one before and leading into the next, each one leaving its mark on our character and identity. Because we are storied people, we often get confused about Scripture. We think that Scripture tells the stories of the heroes of our faith: Abraham, Jacob, Joseph, Moses, Deborah, Rahab, Ruth, David, Peter, Mary Magdalene, Paul. We read the stories in an attempt to emulate their lives or to seek out the moral of their stories. But we need only read the first verse in Genesis to correct this misbegotten view of Scripture: "In the beginning God . . ." Scripture tells the story of God, the one character who was in the beginning and will be into eternity. As Scripture unfolds and more characters are introduced, we learn that the story unfolding in front of our eyes is really the story of a God who is faithful to a broken and hurting creation and how this God invites us, the creation, to participate in the divine story of healing and redemption. With each story we read in Scripture we get a clearer picture of who God is, rather than who each of the characters is.

This approach to reading the grand narrative of Scripture reminds us that we were always intended to find our identity in God and to let our story unfold within God's story. Of course, we are often tempted, like the first character we encounter in Scripture, to write our own story and forge our own identity. "When the woman saw that the fruit of the tree was good for food and pleasing to the eye, and also desirable for gaining wisdom" we find in Genesis 3, "she took some and ate it" (Genesis 3:6). We wonder how many pieces of "fruit" we tend to consume these days, tempted by their glittering promises to help us construct an identity for ourselves that wasn't native to God's purposes. But any identity we might construct outside the life of God is a malformed shadow of who we truly are, who we have been created to be, and how we have been created to relate to our Creator.

In short, identity is formed out of the stories that make up our lives. There's no denying that our communities, our experiences, and our contexts form our identities and that those communities and experiences shape the way we interpret and understand God's image. But as Christians, our contexts are not the whole of the story when it comes to our identity formation. Our story unfolds within God's story, and our identities are formed from God's image.

John Wesley, a theologian whose work has charted the course for many Christians, understood that human image and identity were originally made in God's image along three lines: natural image, which concerns our will, our spiritual nature, and our affections; political image, which reflects God's authority over and care for creation; and moral image, which Wesley understood as that aspect of human life that reflects the righteousness and holiness of God.[1] These reflections of God's image have been distorted, according to Wesley, who also looked to Genesis 3 to tell us the tale of ourselves. In reaching for the fruit of self-construction, Wesley writes, Adam "openly declared that he would no longer have God to rule over him; that he would be governed by his own will, and not the will of Him that created him; and that he would not seek his happiness in God, but in the world, in the works of his hands."[2] Any time we try to create an identity for ourselves, Wesley saw, we find ourselves again reaching for the fruit, making for ourselves an identity in our own image rather than God's image. This, he goes on to say, happens when we are more concerned with *who* we are than *whose* we are.

The pressures to manufacture an identity for ourselves have been present throughout human history but may now be even more of a temptation, complicated by the image-driven culture in which we live. In Barry Schwartz's book *The Paradox of Choice*, he discusses our culture's obsession with self-determination. We believe that through the series of choices we make we can be the authors of our own lives—we can write our own stories and create the best possible identity for ourselves.[3] As a psychologist, Swchartz explains how the inundation of choices and comparisons doesn't lead to greater satisfaction and happiness; it actually leads to helplessness and depression. The even deeper irony with our obsession over choice in a consumer-based society is that the self-authored life is actually being scripted by the image-makers of the culture, such as marketing firms, not the individual.[4]

The evasive allure of the self-authored life often extends to our assumptions about the church. The church we are part of says something about who we are: established, reflective, urban, suburban, casual, social, and so on. Though not always consciously, we select churches for many of the same reasons we select a particular pair of jeans. We are looking for the right fit, style, and comfort. In doing so we enter into a strange "identity triangle" with God, church, and self.

God is the source of all life. The Church, as a sign and symbol of God's kingdom here on earth, is where our self-identity is formed after God's likeness and not the world's. This means the identity of the Church is also formed after the image of God we see in Christ's Body. In order for our lives to have a Christ-shaped identity, we need to participate in the Church. But here is where the triangle gets flipped wrong-side-out: When we decide to be the authors of our own story, we use the Church as one more medium to convey the message about our own identity instead of opening ourselves to be formed by the Church into Christ-likeness. When this happens, the Church is another piece of our self-centered image puzzle, and we are left no better off in terms of finding our true identity than we were when we were attempting to construct it ourselves.

> THOUGH NOT ALWAYS CONSCIOUSLY, WE SELECT CHURCHES FOR MANY OF THE SAME REASONS WE SELECT A PARTICULAR PAIR OF JEANS. WE ARE LOOKING FOR THE RIGHT FIT, STYLE, AND COMFORT.

But individuals are not the only culprits of this misguided identity triangle. Churches can get just as caught up in our image-driven culture. When the church ceases to be a source of Christ-centered identity, it uses the very people it is called to serve to construct an image that is far less than the Body of Christ. For instance, have you ever been a part of a conversation about how to get more young families in the church? If you haven't, you've probably never been to a church board meeting. In fact, young people are often used to this end. The assumption that young families will somehow manufacture an image of a church that is vibrant and full of life is a hoax, not to mention exclusivist and insulting. Only the Holy Spirit can give life to a church. Filling up a Sunday School classroom is not the definitive mark of a Spirit-filled church.

The challenge of identity formation and participation in the church is one that must be taken in the right order if we are going to avoid what we have just described. In other words, if we try to determine our own identities and construct them after something we think we would like to be, we tend to form churches around those very self-constructed identities.

We remember watching a large nondenominational church near us attempt to start a "post-modern church" several years ago. The idea was that you start with the identity of a "post-modern person"—whatever that looked like—and begin building from there. We were saddened to hear a few months later that the attempt had failed, but we were encouraged when the leadership of the church realized that starting with a self-constructed image didn't allow the ministry to call that image into question and was therefore based on a self-constructed image of what a trendy church service looked like rather than God's mission of transforming and redeeming lives. If identity construction becomes the basis of the church's ministry, it really doesn't have much more to offer than a religious mode of maintaining that image.

Identity formation that is found in God's identity, however, is a completely different story. It's a story that begins not with the glittering promise of an alluring fruit that will make us what we think we want to be but rather with "In the beginning God . . ." It is a story that does not begin with who we are but *whose* we are.

## WHO(SE) AM I?

We think there's a lot of hope for young people looking for a place in the church when we determine *whose* we are before we attempt to determine *who* we are. We often get these backwards and then have a really hard time finding a place in the church. We self-identify with all kinds of stories, but until we find ourselves swept up in God's story, we will continue to struggle to find a place in Christ's body. The good news about that is that when we come to find our identity in God's image, it opens up avenues of hospitality and welcome. And when we ask the questions of identity in this order, it means there is no limit to the grace-filled possibilities for making space for artists, writers, poets, and all the others whose unique set of gifts don't fit a traditional model of church ministry.

To borrow from Wesley again, he associates the restoration of our identity with a kind of healing that he calls holiness. "Holiness," he writes, "is no less than the image of God stamped upon the heart; it is no other than the whole mind which was in Christ Jesus," which then "enables us to present our souls and bodies, all we are and all we have, all our thoughts, words, and actions, a continual sacrifice to God." His caveat: "This holiness can have no existence till we are renewed in the image of our mind."[5]

In other words, the hope that Wesley sees, and the hope that we see in regard for those who wonder if they fit in the church is that if our identity is first an association with God's image, then everything else we are becomes an outflow of that identification. In acknowledging that we have given ourselves over to God's grace rather than attempting to construct ourselves, we see that "all we are and all we have," including our unique, storied identities, gifts, and skills, become gifts to the church, opening new and novel possibilities for those gifts being employed for divine, redemptive purposes. When our primary sense of identity is that of belonging to a God whose mission is the redemption and healing of this world, our other sources of self-identity are not erased but repurposed. Rather than serving to define us, they now serve to bring about healing and wholeness to a world in desperate need of both. When our true identity is found in God, those things that previously identified us are redemptively aimed toward ends we never would have previously thought possible.

A challenge for young people today, though, is the temptation to make a fake ID. It's not that only young people are tempted by this, but in contemporary society there have never been so many options open to people to create their own identities. The problem, then, is that the identity we make for ourselves is not the true reality of our Creator's image stamped on our hearts but a bad copy of the real thing. Like the woman in the garden, we are good consumers of those things that promise to give us an identity beyond what we really are and whose identity has been stamped on us at our creation.

Does this mean we need to dismiss all particularity and fade into the background of a congregation? No, because particularity is necessary for community. At the same time, we often struggle to find a place in the church precisely when we submit to the temptation to create our own identity rather than let our identity be found first in the image and story of God and then join our particular gifts, talents, and traits to God's mission of redeeming and healing the world.

In what we've heard in Lynn's story, she struggled to find a place in the church because the church may not have been asking many questions about how the particular identity of a journalist can find a place in God's story. The church knew exactly what to do with a musician on the worship team, but a journalist who has a passion for telling stories in the interest of justice—there really wasn't a Sunday school class or ministry set up for those types. For young artists, musicians, writers, and intellectuals, we suspect that the church may not always know how to find a place for those particular identities, among others, in the God-given mission of healing and redemption in the world, and this can often mean that you sense you don't have a seat at the table in the same way that preachers, prophets, and Sunday School teachers do. The church often struggles to make space in its midst for those whose stories have been formed in ways that the church hasn't seen before.

The good news, however, is that God has a long history of acting in new and surprising ways. We must continue to remember that when God invites someone to join in the divine mission of redeeming the world, it's usually the person we would have least expected. We also must remember that as the church, it would be in the interest of faithfully joining God's redemptive work in the world to seek out creative and novel ways to include those whose stories, skills and passions are different from our own.

The last time we spoke to Lynn, she had begun the process of finding her place in the church. Recognizing that there were many writers in the congregation, her church began to ask about the role of writing in the Christian life and how the art and craft of writing mattered for their life together. A group was assembled, Lynn included, and the church gathered to ask questions of the writers, imagining together how this distinct group could be involved in the church's mission. What was once a mark of self-identity for Lynn has become the means by which she found a place at the table, an aspect of her own identity that is now being explored within the context of a people who see writing not as what makes them who they are but an aspect of faithfully living out the identity of *whose* they are.

Perhaps your storied life doesn't look like many of the other storied lives in your church. Perhaps your storied life doesn't fit as naturally into the age-based ministries or common interest groups of the church as others. Maybe your church knows very well how to include a teacher, construction worker, or accountant into the work God has called your congregation to. But maybe they aren't sure what to do with you, or how your particular story or interests work in the church. And maybe that leaves you wondering if you have a place there at all.

To those who wonder if they have a place in the church, we offer the hope of finding your identity first in Christ. When we show up to the banquet of the church and flash a self-constructed identity, it's nothing more than a fake ID. Not that anyone will deny you entrance necessarily, but an attempt to be authentically present in the church also means authentic submission to be redeemed and transformed in Christ's image. That's a challenge no matter what your age is but one that is especially tough for members of a generation who are told every day that you ought to make the most of yourself, that you can construct your own identity, completely apart from anything else.

Maybe this doesn't sound especially hopeful. Maybe this actually sounds a bit overbearing and not particularly freeing. We would probably share that reaction, too—if God weren't so good. God's story, though, is a story of His faithfulness to redeem this creation, including us. It's not that any other human can restore your true identity, including yourself. As our Creator, God alone can restore that identity and will do it well, perfectly, and completely. When we were created in God's image, it doesn't mean that we all have to look the same, but it does mean that only our Creator can restore that image of holiness when it has fallen to the temptation to be self-constructed. The hope and freedom that paradoxically erupts from submitting ourselves to being redeemed in God's image is that the particular aspects of our storied lives can find new freedom and a new welcome in the church like never before.

To those churches that wonder how to engage young people, we offer the hope of paying careful, relational attention to the distinct and particular identity markers of the young people in your communities. What are the gifts that are offered in that group? What creative and novel ways might those gifts be brought to the table of Christian fellowship and joined to God's mission of healing and redemption? Paying this kind of attention not only engenders practices of hospitality that make our churches more faithfully reflect the kingdom of God, but they also become an important spiritual discipline of humbly and earnestly having eyes to see and ears to hear the new and novel ways that the Spirit is working in our midst. And if the Spirit guides us, we are in good hands no matter how new the territory.

4

# "SPHERELESS"

WHEN WE ARRIVE in a new city, it takes only a matter of minutes to flip through the radio stations and identify the local Christian music affiliate. We don't even have to listen to the lyrics to know that it's contemporary Christian music. It's so obviously not quite like anything else.

Even though Christian music is often intended to make you feel as if you just landed on a pop station to woo you to sit down and stay a while, as a whole, it's never really accomplished this goal. The vocalists are all just a bit too sweet-sounding, the chord progressions slightly predictable, the vocals are always just a bit higher in the mix, and no one loves the acoustic guitar as much as Evangelical Christians.

So once we figure out how to find the Christian station, the NPR station and the country station (Shawna) we're pretty much set.

It's hard to find a better metaphor for the modern American Christian than flipping the radio dial in the car. We tune into the news station when we want to keep up on the events of the world, the Top 40 pop station when we want to know what we are going to be hearing at wedding receptions this summer, and the Christian station when we want a little inspiration or we're craving some good old youth group nostalgia. Our MP3 collection, too, usually resembles this kind of tidy categorization.

Most of the music we have via a worship leader is categorized by genre as "religious." We've also heard a student in our youth group talk about the "God music" she listens to when she needs a bit of an emotional boost. The rest of her MP3s, we presume, are just "regular." When it comes to the radio or iTunes, everything is so separate, so neatly divided, so niched. And so it goes with the culture at large.

MODERN CULTURE HAS NEATLY DIVIDED THE WORLD INTO LOTS OF CLEAR CATEGORIES, AND WE MODERN NORTH AMERICANS ARE USUALLY PRETTY HAPPY WITH THAT.

Modern culture has neatly divided the world into lots of clear categories, and we modern North Americans are usually pretty happy with that. The most recent social networking commercials now highlight that it's easier than ever before to make sure your categories never touch, that you can be sure that this afternoon's status update will be seen by your friends from high school but not your coworkers or your grandparents. We moderns love our categories, even to the point that those of us who identify with some kind of faith background live comfortably with a divide between everything that is "sacred" and everything that is "secular." We're going to call these categories separate "spheres." According to this imaginary divide between the spheres, all religious aspects of life take place in the sacred sphere, and everything else is located in the secular sphere. Church, prayer, and anything having to do with Jesus are neatly categorized in the sacred sphere while work, school, and just about everything else belong to the secular sphere. And for the most part, we moderns like it this way. We like that one sphere doesn't encroach upon another, that we can divide up our lives, and that we have the power of choice to move from one sphere to the other whenever it suits us.

Maybe that kind of convenience is why we began to think of the world in terms of spheres, but perhaps it also began with the purest of intentions, to protect the sacred from the seemingly profane or secular elements of our world we are exposed to as we go about the business of being human.

Regardless of how it happened, the division is neat and tidy. Just as we can flip to a certain radio station, we can flip into a church on

Sunday morning in our nicest jeans and crisp shirt when we want that nice-jeans-and-pressed-shirt kind of experience, or flip into a Saturday night service in our ripped jeans and worn concert T-shirt when that's the kind of church experience we desire. Then we'll flip over to our evening activity revolving around some sort of caffeinated beverage, flip into work the next day, flip home with the roommates or family, constantly adjusting for our surroundings, leaving one station behind to enter another. Before we are even aware of it, fragmentation defines us more than any one of these spheres. There is so little unity to our lives. We're afraid that if we don't tune out of one sphere before we enter another, we'll have quite a cacophony on our hands.

We see this with so many of the teenagers we've worked with over the years. We run into them sitting on the bench outside Dairy Queen with their friends, and as soon as they see us, everything changes: their posture, speech, expression. Or when we're all just hanging out in the youth room and it's time to teach a class, as soon as the Bible comes open, the once chatter-filled room falls silent. Talking about what we did last night is in the secular sphere, but the moment a Bible opens, we've crossed into the sacred sphere, where all things joyful go to be pious and solemn.

This past Christmas Eve we were preparing the service and wondering what we could do that would be a little more creative and engaging to help our congregation be captured by the idea that Christmas is all about light breaking into the darkness. When we thought of starting the service with a standard musical prelude, it didn't seem to live up to the message, so we asked one of our particularly lively teenagers to start the service with a paraphrase of Scripture: "Haven't you heard? Haven't you seen? Light is breaking into the darkness!" We imagined that her usual energy that we saw every week at youth group would be so infectious no one could deny that something good was about to begin. But as soon as she walked into the sanctuary, something happened. Without really being aware of it, she left the secular sphere and entered the sacred sphere, where all excitement is replaced by monotony. We couldn't help but laugh about the result later that night. Neither one of us had ever seen her act so stoic or robotic, but that's what happens, we concluded, when you're taught to think that the sacred has nothing to do with the rest of life.

By this point you have probably guessed we are not making an argument for the preservation of sacred and secular categories. But let's be honest—dividing life that way just makes sense. What is sacred about comparing prices of off-brand cereals or zoning out to a game of Angry Birds? We can't be expected to place the same norms and standards for our activities at work as we do at church, can we?

IF CHURCH IS THE HOME OF THE SACRED, THEN WHY DO SO MANY SINNERS ENTER IT EVERY WEEK? AND IF EVERYTHING OUTSIDE THE CHURCH BUILDING IS SECULAR, WHY DID GOD MAKE IT ALL AND PROCLAIM IT GOOD?

With this sacred-secular divide, we assume that church is the realm of the sacred and everything else is secular—well, maybe with the exception of Christian radio. But if church is the home of the sacred, then why do so many sinners enter it every week? And if everything outside the church building is secular, why did God make it all and proclaim it good?

Reetu's story gives us a different perspective on living a divided life. For Reetu, walking into the church was the riskiest step she's ever taken.

## A GIRL CROSSES THE STREET

Reetu had never stepped foot in a church before she was a teenager. As a young girl in India, she was taken on a field trip to look at the architecture of a church building, but they never actually went inside. And why would she go into a Christian church? Reetu and her family lived firmly in the cultural and religious sphere of India; they were Sikh. Their religious practices embodied their cultural identity. They celebrated festivals of Indian gods, and they spoke and sang in their native tongue.

In India, "You assume every white person is Christian," Reetu told us. Since she wasn't white, since she hadn't been in a church, since nothing about her looked like the Christians she knew, she couldn't possibly have crossed into their world.

When Reetu was in the eighth grade her family moved to a small town in Michigan, where, for the first time in her life, she was surrounded by white people.

"We *were* the diversity in that town," she said. And as if it weren't difficult enough to be the only family who wasn't white, in a high school graduating class of only thirty-three students, she stood out.

But Reetu adjusted to the rhythms of a new culture quickly. She found it was easy to be Indian at home and American just about everywhere else. Living in two worlds had its challenges, but she learned how to slip back and forth between the distinct cultural spheres with ease.

Across the street from the store her father owned and operated was a Baptist church. The little old white ladies from the church would frequent the store—always friendly and polite, always with an invitation for Reetu's family to attend church services. The invitations began to come so frequently that Reetu's dad came to the family one evening suggesting that perhaps some appeasement would make the invitations stop. "You will go with your mother to one of these church services so they will stop asking us to come to church," he said to the family.

Soon after, Reetu stepped inside a church for the first time. It was a Sunday morning service, and she was there with her family, who didn't venture too far into such unfamiliar territory. Taking the very back pew, Reetu and her family had in mind that they were doing nothing more than simply fulfilling an obligation, hoping this would put an end to the invitations.

Reetu didn't understand much of what was said in the service—she just remembers it was quite boring. After the service one of the ladies suggested that she attend Sunday School, a prospect that was anything but appealing to the young teenager. Reetu didn't need to use words when she looked up at her mother and pleaded for a way out of the invitation.

Apparently, words would have been more effective. "Sure, she can go," responded her mother, determined to do whatever it took to put to bed once and for all the pestering invitations to attend church, sacrificing an hour of her daughter's comfort for the hope of ending all further awkward conversations.

The only problem was that once she tried Sunday School, Reetu enjoyed it quite a bit. "I really liked it," she recalled as she shared with us about her first experience with church and her decision to continue attending Sunday School with the little group of Baptists down the street. Her parents didn't have a problem with her desire to attend, because like many nominally religious folk, they assumed religion isn't much more than a collection of some nice morals that would help their daughter become a good and kind person. As she crossed the street week after week and entered the church building, her family didn't imagine she was truly leaving their world and entering an altogether different sphere. She would always be Indian, always be Sikh. And since this was the case, sending Reetu to church on a weekly basis was a great way not to have to deal with the incessant invitations to attend church.

That's the way life was for a few years. Reetu went to church, but she didn't really consider herself a Christian. Christians were white, and she wasn't white. Christians lived a certain way, and that wasn't the way she lived. Her home life was a cloister of her Indian culture in the midst of the white American world around her. Her father was strict and kept her from engaging in too many outside activities. She had never been allowed to attend sleepovers at other girls' homes or engage in the other activities that so many of the American kids were doing.

So when she asked her father if she could attend a weekend overnight event with the Baptist church's youth group, she already knew the answer. In fact, Reetu wasn't even sure she wanted to attend when she asked her father, but she knew it wouldn't matter. His answer was sure to be a firm no. Nervously, she decided to ask his permission anyway, and to her surprise his answer was a simple "Sure, you can go."

The event was a fairly typical American Evangelical youth revival: loud bands, eccentric speakers, Christian kitsch plastered on walls, booths, and bodies, and lots of adrenaline-pumped adolescents. Right on cue, in the Saturday evening service one of the speakers invited the students to pray a prayer of salvation and give their lives to Christ, the kind of prayer that most church kids have heard at nearly every youth event they've ever attended, the kind that sounded as if the speaker had found it in the back of an outdated evangelism pamphlet. But Reetu prayed the prayer anyway.

That night she sat in her bedroom and thought, *Oh no—I'm a Christian. What am I going to do?* When she remembered her thoughts from that night, Reetu told us it never occurred to her that she could hide the fact that she had given her life to Christ. She didn't realize, as so many American youth do, that she could go home and live as if it had never happened. It never occurred to her that she could simply place the experience in a quiet category of her life and go on in every other sphere as if she hadn't committed to something real. It didn't occur to her to live her life in spheres.

THAT NIGHT REETU SAT IN HER BEDROOM AND THOUGHT, *OH NO—I'M A CHRISTIAN. WHAT AM I GOING TO DO?*

Reetu was painfully aware that a real change had taken place in her, and as she continued to reflect on what she had done, she became more and more aware that when she left her house and walked across the street, her commitment wasn't one that would allow her to leave home at home and to leave church at church. Her commitment was the kind that claimed her whole. There were no neat divisions, no categories, no fragmentation. This commitment would affect everything.

Reetu knew she had to tell her parents, but she decided to wait until she was eighteen and legally free of any control her parents might try to impose. Over the next few months, she convinced her parents to let her attend a nearby Christian college, using the argument that it had a strong nursing program, knowing they valued the sciences and would be proud to tell their friends their daughter was a nurse.

After they had agreed and Reetu had been accepted to the nursing program and made her move to campus, she began to experience a strange sense of freedom. Attending a Christian school meant she could live openly and that everyone could know that she was a Christian. But that sense of wholeness disappeared with every trip home. In making trips between campus and her family's house, Reetu still lived a double life: at home one way, at school another. It wasn't much different than days of crossing the street from home to church and the line between Indian and American culture.

Just before the spring break during her freshman year, Reetu turned eighteen and headed home for the week, determined to tell her parents that Christ had changed her life. It was more difficult than she anticipated to communicate her faith to them. "My Christianity was American," she said. "I had talked about my faith only in English and never my own language, so I didn't know how to tell them."

Somehow, though, Reetu found the words to tell her parents that she was a Christian and was surprised by their calm reaction. "No, you're not really a Christian," they responded cooly. "You don't know what you're talking about." Though their words were calm, Reetu sensed there was something deeper underneath their reaction, and she began to fear for her safety.

Picking up her phone, she chose the first name that came to mind and called her former Sunday School teacher, who came and picked her up from her house, which only enraged her father, who began incessantly calling Reetu's phone. When she found the courage to answer his calls, he began to threaten that if she didn't come home, he would kill himself and her family.

What had she done? In one conversation Reetu had endangered her entire family. She knew she might be at some risk, but she had not considered that sharing her faith would put her family in any kind of danger. Terrified, Reetu called the police, shakily explaining the situation as best she could. But when she went home to meet with her parents under police protection, her parents convinced her to tell the officers that it was actually the church members who had kidnapped her and that her family never gave her reason to run.

During the remainder of that spring break, Reetu felt the walls of the old sphere in which she once lived closing in on her. Would she be allowed to return to school? If not, would she ever find another place where she could live openly as a Christian without fear of her family? Finally, Reetu's mother and uncle convinced her father of the value of completing the school semester.

At the end of the traumatic break, Reetu headed back to campus, certain that whatever options the summer would present, returning home would not be among them. After connecting with a few members of the staff at her university, she learned that there was an opportunity to spend her summer working with a mission organization based in El Paso, Texas. She filed the necessary paperwork, made the necessary connections, and raised the money she needed to be able to spend her summer hundreds of miles from home. She worked hard to finish the semester and somehow quickly completed her work before boarding a southbound flight to El Paso.

When she arrived in El Paso, everything felt different. The air was dry and hot, and the people looked and lived very differently than the Americans she knew in Michigan. Meeting her contact at the airport, they made the short trip to the church she would call home for the next several weeks of summer. About thirty other college students began arriving at the church that afternoon, each destined for various mission destinations. They were grouped into teams according to where they would be going, but because Reetu's situation was a bit of a special arrangement, she was neither preparing to travel to her summer home, nor did she have a team to join. She enjoyed the company of so many others who were so understanding of her situation but was still a bit apprehensive about what the summer would bring once all of her colleagues departed for their destinations.

After the last student had left for the airport and the church was empty, Reetu felt the beginnings of a profound loneliness, wondering if there was anywhere she could belong. Within a few days, she made contact with the congregation that would become her local church, a small but lively and welcoming Hispanic church in El Paso. There, a scared young Indian woman who had spent her life adapting to American culture found the peace of Christ in the welcome she received from people who were again new to her. Reetu fell in love with the church there, and they loved her back.

"Every week I was in someone's home," she recalls. Sharing meals and life stories, Reetu became a part of this church family despite language and cultural barriers. "Even though none of my friends were there, I loved it. I didn't feel I was missing anything."

The summer ended too quickly. Reetu insisted it wasn't necessary, but the church took up a love offering for her anyway. They simply wanted to send her back with some of the richness her company had brought to their fellowship.

When she finally reconnected with her parents, they acted as if nothing had ever happened, as if Reetu had never prayed that prayer, never stepped out of a sphere-based life, never brought shame on the family, never changed. It was the flimsy kind of denial that puts true peace on hold.

Still, Reetu couldn't get away from the sense that she was no longer defined by spheres, that her Christian faith made a whole claim upon her life, and that this claim was even extending to her education and career, which meant changing her major from nursing to cross-cultural missions. As long as her parents believed Reetu was training to be a nurse, her education would be seen as worthwhile. Conversations about religion were easy to avoid. Their Indian friends and relatives didn't have to know this embarrassing secret about their daughter. They could hide the fact that she had become a Christian, especially if they could boast that their daughter was a nurse. But if she were to become a missionary, like the white people who built those American-looking churches over in India, what would they tell people? She would bring disgrace on the whole family. That conversation could wait for now, Reetu decided.

Back at school, Reetu experienced a new kind of freedom. For the first time in her life, she wasn't living between two worlds. Her parents knew she was a Christian, and she was back in an environment in which she felt safe to be a Christian. No more hiding. She didn't have to cross the street to leave one sphere and enter another. Christ's sphere encompassed her entire life, and she knew what she had to do.

Reetu had never been baptized. Baptism had been explained to her as an outward sign of her inward faith. But that was exactly the problem: her faith had always been inward, hidden away to protect herself and her family from disgrace. When she returned to school that fall, Reetu didn't want to hide her faith in some kind of inward spiritual realm or sacred sphere. She was ready to live a life free of spheres, to move beyond the fragmentation of her previous life and to live in a sense of wholeness.

Reetu prepared for baptism in a small church near the campus in which she had become an active member. She had been waiting years to take part in this sacrament and receive the grace of God waiting for her in the waters of baptism, but something always held her back. Part of her life had always been trapped in another sphere. On the day of her baptism, Reetu shared her story with the congregation before entering the water, saying to the onlooking congregation, "I know I am finally free to tell everyone that I am a Christian." As she entered the waters and they enveloped her entirely, fragmentation gave way to wholeness.

SHE HAD BEEN WAITING YEARS TO TAKE PART IN THIS SACRAMENT AND RECEIVE THE GRACE OF GOD WAITING FOR HER IN THE WATERS OF BAPTISM.

## A WORLD OF NO SPHERES

When we heard Reetu's story, we couldn't help but think about the hope that it offered to those who were wondering if the church still had room for them, asking if they still belong in the church at all. Most of the time when we listen to people explain that they don't feel as if they belong in the church, it has something to do with a fragmented life. We hear about the church being such a separate sphere that it has no bearing whatsoever upon the other areas of life, and the church becomes hopelessly irrelevant. Why stick with something that asks so much but has so little to do with the real world?

Here's where we think the hope is: the real world is a world where there are no spheres at all. The reality we see is a world that isn't fragmented but a world that is a whole reality. In other words, all the world belongs to God. Work, friends, family, school—all of it—is a whole reality, and none remains completely separate from the other. The hope for us is that our lives can take on a holistic character, that faith is no longer relegated to a dusty, irrelevant sphere of life but becomes an all-consuming reality that helps heal the fragmentation that tends to mark our lives.

If we could get ancient for a moment, we think that a man from long ago has something to say to us today about this kind of modern, sphered, fragmented life. Augustine was a man who struggled with living his life in spheres. His faith lived in one sphere, but his desires lived in a completely different sphere. He was a man who struggled with unchecked desires for material, for glory, for respect, for sex. But as he grew, prayed, and studied, he came to the realization that the world was not divided into spheres but that it was a complete totality, and that totality all belonged to God. All the world is created good by God, he said, and as Christians we ought to love the world in that respect. We ought to think that the way we engage things like economics and justice are divine enterprises, because justice doesn't live in a separate sphere from faith in Christ. Politics, food, art, love, work, money, sex—all of it comes as part of a whole creation, and as a whole creation we ought to deeply love the world, longing for its healing and redemption. It all has to do with our faith. There is nothing that isn't claimed by our faith in the goodness of God, because nothing lives in a separate sphere from God's goodness.

Of course, Augustine realized that there are times when our desires for some of the good things of creation can eclipse our desire for God, and that's when we tend to get into trouble, but as long as we get the idea that the world is a whole totality and that our primary desire is for God, things will tend to work themselves out.

Christians in North America could learn quite a bit from Augustine. We have become quite proficient at living as if the world is a collection of spheres rather than a whole totality, and we've become good at crossing between the distinct and separate spheres in our lives. There's something a bit jarring to us about Reetu's story, especially when it's placed in this modern, North American context. When we hear her story against that background, we're reminded that many of us tend to live fragmented lives—that we think faith is relegated to a completely separate "sacred-religious sphere" and that life in Christ's sphere presents no real danger for most of us living in North America. We are not at risk of losing our families, being disowned, causing harm to those we love; we simply find it more convenient to draw a line between our sacred and secular lives.

Of course, this propensity to live in spheres didn't come out of nowhere. There is actually a long history behind these ideas that involves the same philosophical discussions that placed humanity at the center of what it means "to be." Once we made that move, it meant that God has being only insofar as we humans believe in God. In this way of thinking, it's actually our human belief that allows God to exist at all. Our intellectual framework, or our way of thinking, trapped God in our experience, made God our intellectual puppet or imaginary friend.

However, in doing so, this God we claimed to "believe in" was no longer free to enter our "secular lives." This God was not really bigger than us and could not call us to be anything truly bigger than we already are. We tamed a wild, all-encompassing God to become a being in our own image whom we could choose to meet in a few selected places and times, like church on a Sunday. That's where God lives—but nowhere else.

Eighteenth-century German philosopher Immanuel Kant considered it "a scandal of philosophy and universal human reason that the existence of things outside us . . . should be assumed merely on faith, and that if it occurs to anyone to doubt it, we should be unable to answer him with a satisfactory proof."[1] In other words, Kant, along with the Western world, came to a point in which we were so self-consumed that we could not recognize the existence of anything beyond our humanity. If anything were to exist at all, it existed only in our own experience and imagination. We thought so much of our own ability to reason that we could not even comprehend a thing that we did not invent ourselves.

But again, we think this kind of thinking tends to lead us toward a really difficult situation for people in this generation who are wondering if the church has a place for them. If we go the route of Kant and the rest who might describe life in terms of relegating certain aspects of life to certain "spheres," it means that our faith lives in a sphere that is totally separate from some of the things in life that mean the most to us. If justice for the poor and oppressed has nothing to do with our faith, you can be sure that this is the result of thinking of our lives in terms of spheres.

Gladly, the God whom the Christian Church confesses, the Creator of heaven and earth, is bound to no such categories or experiences, no few places and times. Heaven and earth, things seen and unseen, the spiritual and the physical, have all been created by God. All of it matters to Christians, because Christians are that group of people who don't live fragmented lives. Christians are that strange group of people who think the whole world has something to do with the God we believe in—or in other words, life in the church is where we come to realize that there is no such thing as secular! There are no spheres.

Reetu's story gives us a glimpse into a world seen rightly. It's a world in which there are no separate spheres, and her ability to find a place in the church, we think, has a lot to do with her ability to live a life without spheres. The faith in God she has found in the church isn't relegated to a separate sphere, and therefore it matters. Her faith is refreshingly relevant, because it isn't private, separate, and removed from the things that matter most. Instead, her faith is really and radically connected to all aspects of life. Her career, her family, her academic future—her faith touches everything. And what's even more hopeful to us about her story is that as a person who was relatively new to North America, she didn't even see an option to keep her faith in a separate sphere. For Reetu, it was never a possibility that a commitment to Christ didn't matter for every aspect in life. For her, the sacred presence of God spills into every part of life, and that, we think, is an exciting and hopeful way to see the world. There is nothing in heaven or on earth God did not create or God does not give life to. Therefore, there is nothing kept from God.

THERE IS NOTHING IN HEAVEN OR ON EARTH GOD DID NOT CREATE OR GOD DOES NOT GIVE LIFE TO. THEREFORE, THERE IS NOTHING KEPT FROM GOD.

## GETTING WET AND SEEING THE WORLD RIGHT

Another aspect of Reetu's story that gives us hope for those who are looking for a place in the church is the way in which she engaged so deeply in the strange practices of the church. These are the practices of baptism and Communion the church calls sacraments, a name that suggests these practices are indeed sacred but not that they need to be relegated to a private, sacred sphere of life.

In fact, the sacraments are a perfect example of the absurdity of our categories of sacred and secular. In Reetu's story, and for Christians everywhere, baptism is a symbol by which we once and for all leave behind a fragmented world and start living in the all-encompassing reality of Christ's salvation. Even the imagery of baptism suggests that there is nothing about life that remains unaffected. When we go into the waters of baptism, there isn't a part of us that doesn't get wet, and we love that about baptism. We come out soaking wet, having been completely submerged under the grace-filled waters of the baptistery, and that suggests to us that our whole lives are touched by baptism. Baptism signifies we are claimed whole by Christ. Nothing stays dry.

The sacraments also suggest that there is a rupture between the sacred and the secular because the things that the sacraments use are so *ordinary*. Certainly, there is pomp and ceremony that surround the sacraments, and that's because they are sacred. But at the same time, think about how ordinary everything involved in the sacraments is. Water is the most plentiful compound in our bodies, most of our planet is covered by it, and when we decide it's going to be our drink of choice at dinner, we tell the server that we want "just water." What could be more seemingly un-sacred than plain old water?

Even baptism appears no different than taking a bath, one of the most routine and uncelebrated aspects of life. What's so special about cleaning our bodies? As people in youth ministry, we do recognize that a bath can be a bit sacred, especially after a week at camp, but really, taking a bath probably ranks up there with flossing—it's something that needs to be done, but it isn't really all that special. What is holy about taking a dip?

Likewise, Communion couldn't really use more boring elements. The bread never tastes that great. What is more common than bread? At least once a week we have to throw out bread from our house because it became either stale or moldy. And we'll admit—we often let our dog have the heel of the loaf because we just don't like it as much as the soft inside slices. The Communion bread is plain, it's usual, and it's bland.

Similarly, wine was the most common beverage to share with a meal in Jesus' day. If you're from a tradition that uses wine at Communion, even the wine is fairly uninventive. A friend of ours who was from a grape juice tradition took a class on the sacraments once. The professor was going to use wine at Communion and gave our friend instructions to go to the store and get some wine for it. Not knowing what wine was supposed to be used, our friend said that he chose what he assumed was a relatively nice dinner wine. When he returned, the professor laughed and said, "Dinner wine? This is too fancy! We need communion wine." Plain is what is required.

The elements of the sacraments are plain. They are not sacred in and of themselves, and that's precisely the point. In our use of them, we are reminded that the sacred and the secular are never separated. In our celebration of the sacraments, the most sacred practices of the Church, we use some of the plainest things available to us. But at the same time, we believe that God's sacred grace is entirely present through those completely plain things. In the sacraments we are reminded that the plain and divine have been forever joined by God's becoming human and that as the people who believe in a God who became flesh, we do not try to create a "secular sphere" in which God has no authority.

At baptism we ask the Holy Spirit to come and be present over the water, hovering over the face of the deep, and our memories are triggered to hold in mind the way the Spirit hovered over the waters of the deep at creation (Genesis 1:2), bringing order to chaos, wholeness to fragmentation. When we invoke the presence of the Holy Spirit, when we claim Christ's life, death, and resurrection as our own and ask the Father to create us anew, we come up from those waters a different person, a new creation. Order is brought to chaos, and our lives are brought to wholeness from fragmentation. It's not just getting dunked in a swimming pool. God chooses to use the ordinary things of this world to make a whole claim on us and to redeem our fragmented lives, allowing us to live whole lives by the virtue of God's whole claim upon us in baptism.

We love the fact that Reetu's story includes the sacraments so boldly, because the sacraments remind us over and over that the sacred has invaded every inch of this profane and sinful world. Her story helps us see the world as it really is: a God-created totality rather than a bunch of unrelated spheres that shouldn't touch one another. As we continue to gather around the sacraments, our worship gives us the eyes to see creation as it really is, undivided, without lines and categories. The sacraments are the practices of the Church that bring this reality to life for us.

Reetu's story helps us see more clearly that we too often have lives that are fragmented between spheres. The next time you have the opportunity to receive the elements of Communion, we challenge you to remember the kind of reality they signify. When you receive them, remember that there are no spheres but that in receiving the gifts of God you receive a whole life, healed of fragmentation. Reetu's baptism into the Church, too, signaled the end of her journey back and forth between spheres and marked the beginning of her journey toward a whole life under Christ's authority.

As for culture, please recognize that this story is not about giving up one's cultural identity in order to become a version of cultureless Christianity. And we certainly are not implying that Reetu had to give up her Indian identity for a more American culture of Christianity. There is no uncontextualized, culture-free way to live in Christ. Often when we think we can separate our faith from those particular things that distinguish who we are, we end up assuming that Christianity inherently implies the norms of our culture that we don't always even notice. American Christians are often guilty of this, and we write this as members of the guilty party. Later we're going to talk a bit more about the notion of particularity and how it can be a vital means of hope for those who are struggling to find a place in the church.

## A PLACE FOR THE SPHERELESS

For now, though, we hope that Reetu's story has been able to offer you as much hope as it's offered to us. We hope you've been able to see the way in which her commitment to Christ was never something that she was able to stash in a religious sphere, away from her family and career life, but that it was a commitment that grasped her whole. And that kind of commitment is the kind that affects the way someone engages the church. It means that as we wonder if there is a place for us in a church that doesn't seem to have much room for young people, we are reminded that the church doesn't exist in a separate sphere from the rest of life, and we can't abandon it on the grounds of its seeming to be irrelevant to all other areas of life. At the same time, we can also remind the church that all those things that it sometimes tends to forget are the things that make it appear so irrelevant at times and cannot be separated from its life and its mission. The things that grasp our imagination as a young generation and make us passionate are the things that do not belong to a separate secular sphere while the church goes on its way of living in a sacred, religious sphere. And often the church needs a young generation to remind it of that. The church needs those who will engage it with the understanding that God's mission of redemption and healing extends to all corners of the earth.

The church stands in need of people like Reetu, who at times felt as if there wasn't a strong connection between the things that were going on in the world and the "sacred, religious" sphere that her church seemed to think it lived in. She saw hurt in the world, and as one who couldn't see the world as being divided into spheres, she was a Christian who knew that she needed to engage the world. And sometimes that can be a bit alien in a church and a culture that assumes that the church and culture occupy different spheres. A final piece of Reetu's story will help to highlight what we're talking about.

One summer during college, Reetu and her friends from the Baptist church did what they did every Wednesday night throughout high school—they went to church. But this time they arrived at church as adults rather than high schoolers and were told they were too old to go in with the youth.

So they went into the adult Bible study. Reetu remembers that it wasn't the kind of place they felt comfortable sharing their thoughts, passions, dreams, or asking questions, so they sat quietly and listened. The next week, as always, they went to the church. But this time they abandoned the adult class, quietly slipped into the sanctuary, and began talking about life, Scripture, prayer, and the way their faith connected with their passion to reach out to a world in need. When one of the women in the church found them sitting in seclusion away from the adult class, she asked what they were doing. After Reetu and her friends explained they were having their own sort of informal Bible study, the woman tried to tell them as kindly as she knew that they were not qualified to lead a Bible study and that they simply could not hold their own Bible study in the church. If gathering together around Scripture was what they wanted, they would have to join the adult group.

The disconnect, we think, was more than just a lack of understanding or tact, but at a deeper level it was about a group of young people who wanted to explore the ways their faith was profoundly connected to the real issues of a world in need, a world that God had created good, now groaning for redemption. But in a world of spheres, what does faith have to do with the world? Does a holy enclave of Christians gathered in a church on a Wednesday night have anything to do with poverty, teen suicide, homelessness, sexual abuse, lack of education, health care, or food? Those are, after all, things that don't belong in the sacred/religious sphere. Those are secular issues.

What saddens us is that when we asked what happened to that little group, Reetu told us a story we've heard too many times: many went back to school and haven't been back to church, some stayed out of sheer guilt, and others hung around because they just weren't sure what else to do. For some of her group, the church, which saw the world in spheres, didn't have room for those who want their deep faith in Christ to touch the deep need of the world.

We're guessing that if you're reading this book, you might resonate with this kind of deep desire to let your faith loose to impact the world and a church that isn't sure it knows what to do with you. If you at all resonate with that idea, we are hopeful that Reetu has something to offer us. She has the ability to see the world as a whole totality, all created by God and in need of our attention as followers of Jesus. She has the ability to see that the world is not divided into spheres and that her faith does matter to the issues of the world, so much so that she is using her education to train for work in the inner city of Indianapolis to address some of the concerns we addressed earlier. And she does it as a person who realizes that Christ has a whole claim on her life.

Flipping from one station to the next, from one web site to another, from this app to that text message—it's the most natural thing in the world. It's the way we live; so separating our lives into neat categories that allow us to flip from one to the next might seem natural. Keeping the things that are sacred safe from all that is secular makes sense. But that isn't the faith of people who follow Christ. The faith of Christians is faith that God has forever joined the sacred and the secular, that Jesus is Lord of everything, and that there are no

THE FAITH OF CHRISTIANS IS FAITH THAT GOD HAS FOREVER JOINED THE SACRED AND THE SECULAR, THAT JESUS IS LORD OF EVERYTHING, AND THAT THERE ARE NO SPHERES.

spheres. If we believe what we confess as Christians, that God is the Creator of the heavens and the earth, there is no need to draw lines between sacred and secular—it's all God's!

This isn't good news only for a world in need, but also for those who wonder if the church has room for them, their deep desire to engage a broken world, and their hope to participate in God's redemption of creation. First, our participation in the church is where we are formed and shaped to see what is true, that the world is not separate spheres. Our worship, our gathering around the special practices of the church called sacraments, teaches us to see the world right, to be capable of envisioning the world as a whole, and to let the hope of God's redemption touch every part of our world. Second, it enlivens and emboldens those who wonder about their place in the church to be faithfully present in their churches and to remind their churches that the world Christians see is not a world of spheres but that our divine calling is to engage in God's mission of redeeming the entire world. In this respect, the church stands in deep need of young people who are willing to engage them in this way and to let their lives be a living witness to the fact that God's desire is for the redemption of the whole world—not just an imaginary religious sphere.

# A
# TEA PARTY
5    FOR
# TWO

ONE OF THE most painful things we have experienced in youth ministry is when students cut themselves off. They decide they are done
with church, done with God, done with us, and just disappear. This
is even more painful for us than seeing moral failures or counseling
families through divorce, because as long as a teen stays engaged and
is willing to talk with us and their brothers and sisters in Christ, we
know there's hope.

The church community is a means of grace, and the Holy Spirit
uses these interactions to move us closer to the Father. But when one
of our teenagers completely cuts himself or herself off, it feels hopeless.
Nothing is impossible for God, but some teenagers have become experts at avoiding grace. They block anyone associated with the church
from their Facebook page, change their cell phone numbers, and tell
their siblings to inform us that they are not home if we visit. We just
want them to know and see the truth of God's love for them, but they
won't hear it.

It's hard to build relationships with people who won't talk to you.
Then there are people who are more than willing to talk but make

it awfully hard to be heard. Honest conversations in the church are so important, yet we are often so bad at them. We either avoid hard conversations in the name of "love," or we use heated rhetoric to ram one another in the name of "truth." Speaking the truth in love, as the apostle Paul commands, sometimes seems to be beyond our grasp, but for the church, conversations that speak truth in love are never truly out of reach, because the church is composed by the presence of the Holy Spirit. Where the Holy Spirit is, our broken humanity finds divine potential.

Consider Kassidy's story. A young man basically raised in the pews, now in his late twenties, has seen the gift of the Spirit in action through Christian conversation. After seeing the potential Christians have, he still struggles with the reality of the state of discourse in the wider Christian community. While he has found a place in the church locally, he has some reservations about his place in a larger denomination. Still, he is open to see where his own heart and actions need to be confronted as he strives to be more like Christ. His story fascinated us, though, and we learned a lot from listening to the way it opened up hope for the church to be a place of redemption and healing for a young man who wondered if the church still had a place for him.

You could say that Kassidy is a member of a "legacy" family in his home church in southern California. His grandparents, parents, brothers and sisters, and now he and his wife and their little girl, have all played significant roles in the life of his church. Going to church was never an option; it was a given. "It was like school," Kassidy told us. "Unless you're puking or bleeding, you're going." But that certainly didn't mean his place in the church was a given for life.

Whether it was Sunday School, Vacation Bible School, youth group, or Sunday night services, Kassidy was a fixture at any and all church events. He might have been breaking some piece of church furniture, concocting new jokes about his youth pastor's baldness, or being a general nuisance, but he was always taking part in the children's and youth ministry events, whether the adult leaders wanted him or not.

When Kassidy graduated from high school, it was for him, like so many other young adults, a time of major life changes. His church, too, was also going through a difficult season of transition. Leaving the youth group and entering his twenties made a big impact on Kassidy's sense of community, as there wasn't the natural, structural, built-in ministry for him to connect with in the church. Growing up in the children's ministry and transitioning to the youth ministry gave him a community for every stage of life, but when high school came to a conclusion, the idea of transitioning to the adult ministries was daunting. What would happen to his community of friends that had come to mean so much to him and was so able to connect with what he was going through?

Throughout his high school years, he and his sister, Kaydee, had developed a close group of Christian friends in the church who helped him think through and live out his faith. "Growing up," Kassidy recalls, "we always hung out with our group of friends from grade school through high school and had these great talks about things. But as we grew older and spread out, we lost that connection." Kaydee was still in high school, and his friends were moving away or simply growing apart. Simultaneously, Kassidy was wrestling with this loss of community, the changes at his church, and the growing sense that there wasn't really a natural place for him there anymore.

In the midst of all of this, Kassidy and his girlfriend, Jenn, began to grow more distant from the church. The problems they saw in the church, the changes, and the lack of place all seemed to be a bit too much to draw them to connect in the way they once had. It wasn't long before Kassidy's mom noticed and talked to him about it. "You don't leave your church because there are problems," she said to him in a conversation about the church. "You help to fix the problems."

Kassidy wasn't entirely convinced by his mom's logic, but he finally gave in to her petitions, and he and Jenn paid a visit to the newly formed college group their church had just started.

As observers to the new ministry and everything else that was happening in the church, they were skeptical at first, testing the waters and wading in slowly. But they were surprised by what they found. There was something very real about the group. There was scripture, there was worship, and there was fellowship in authentic community—everything Kassidy had been missing. "It was a lot of just living life together and talking about what was going on in our lives," Kassidy said. The lost sense of place and the sadness of losing community were soon replaced by the significant connections that Kassidy and Jenn found in the college group.

Of course, being surprised by finding such a good thing in the church was also a bit challenging. He remembered his mom's words about engaging problems in his church rather than running from them, and he became convinced that there was something substantial to what she had said to him that day. Kassidy began to pray about the problems in the church and to posture himself to meet the challenges his church was facing in a difficult time of transition. Again, he was surprised when God started answering his prayers and the whole environment of the congregation began to shift.

As their relationship progressed, Kassidy and Jenn announced their engagement and stayed connected to their college group. The church welcomed a new pastor with whom Kassidy developed a trusting and respectful relationship. He was experiencing the life of Christian community he had been missing.

But life was about to take a fast turn for Kassidy and Jenn. About a year before their scheduled wedding, the couple got some news that would change everything: they were pregnant—and shocked. Kassidy was embarrassed and didn't know how his family would respond. He told his parents first, who were incredibly gracious and supportive. Then it was time to tell Kaydee. She couldn't bring herself to talk to Kassidy when he broke the news to her. Was she mad, disappointed, confused? Kassidy couldn't guess what was going on in her mind, especially considering all that was going on in his. After sharing the news with his sister, Kassidy endured a long and awkward week of her silence.

It was during that week that Adam and Wendy, the leaders of the college group, called up Kassidy and Jenn and invited them over for dinner. "You don't have to tell us anything," Kassidy remembers Adam saying as they sat around the dinner table. "We don't have to talk about any of this stuff if you don't want to—we just want to love on you guys." Both leaders seemed to live the perfect life. They each worked a full-time job while raising three kids, and now they had actually taken the step of inviting Kassidy and Jenn's chaos into their own serenity. Their invitation was more than a meal; it was an invitation to actually receive the uncertainty, fear, and anxiety of Kassidy's situation into their own lives, to make a place for a frightened young couple in a time of deep need. Their hospitality, Kassidy remembers, spoke to him and Jenn in ways that words could not.

THEIR INVITATION WAS MORE THAN A MEAL; IT WAS AN INVITATION TO ACTUALLY RECEIVE THE UNCERTAINTY, FEAR, AND ANXIETY OF KASSIDY'S SITUATION INTO THEIR OWN LIVES

Kassidy wasn't entirely sure how the news would be received by the rest of the college group, but he did know that after talking with Adam and Wendy, he and Jenn needed to tell the group what was going on in their lives sooner rather than later. How could they not share something like this with those who had been so authentic with them and who had become such a real means of God's grace? As Kassidy suspected, the group was loving and supportive when he and Jenn made the news known at the weekly gathering. Their reaction, Kassidy remembers, was something he would have expected Jesus to do, and if he was honest with himself, it was the kind of reaction he had really come to expect from his group. What he didn't expect was the conversation that began to unfold after he and Jenn shared the news. People started to share and ask questions and open up about their own life experiences. Perhaps most unexpected of all, in the midst of this safe and loving conversation, Kaydee began to talk to her brother for the first time in over a week. The open, honest discussion among a community of Christian believers broke down the walls of silence and distrust, restoring a broken and hurting relationship.

Nine months later, the entire college group crammed onto the church platform alongside grandparents, Mom and Dad, brothers and sisters, as Kassidy and Jenn dedicated their daughter to the Lord.

Today Kassidy and Jenn find themselves at another awkward point of transition. In their late twenties and parents to a five-year-old daughter, they have outgrown the college group, but they haven't outgrown their desire for authentic Christian community. With two full-time jobs, a kindergartner in school, and a pile of homework to complete for his B.A. in religion, Kassidy will tell you that it's awfully hard to find space and time for significant fellowship. "When we were kids, we had down time, and that down time had to be filled," he told us. "Now, Jenn and I can only pray for that down time."

Even in the absence of the community they once had, Kassidy and Jenn are trying to be intentional about staying involved and building new relationships. They serve as youth sponsors in the youth group, and Kassidy was recently voted to the church board, a move that left some of his former Sunday School teachers stunned speechless. Kassidy and his mom drive together to board meetings, and we hope that she'll continue to challenge him the same way she did at the last point of transition. Conversations like that are priceless.

## TALKING POLITICS

One of the things Kassidy appreciated about the college group was his ability to be honest about his thoughts, questions, and opinions, even when those opinions were at odds with the rest of the group. He often found that his opinions, especially in politics, were a bit out of the norm, but that was fine with the college group. He could disagree with them and still know he was loved, still know that his politics were just as much an expression of his desire to be a faithful Christian in the world as it was for the rest of the members of the community who held different views. Without a group like that, it became difficult to know where and when the appropriate times to process some big issues with fellow believers were.

In 2008 California was in an upheaval over Proposition 8, a controversy that did not remain in the legislative halls of the state but were felt in California's churches as well. The California Supreme Court had recently ruled in favor of same-sex marriage. Prop 8 was on the ballot as a constitutional amendment that would define marriage as an institution entered into only by a man and woman. The political action groups were all geared up for a big fight, and most churches joined the fray.

In the midst of the heated political climate, a close male friend confided in Kassidy that he had strong feelings of attraction toward men and expressed his pain and fear with the situation, not knowing where else to turn. He hadn't acted on his feelings or made any life-changing decisions, but he was just looking for a safe person to talk to and process, one who wouldn't add to the pain or confusion. Kassidy had a lot of questions, but he knew he needed to show love to this friend who had already been mistreated by others in whom he had confided.

At the height of the political debate, Kassidy's church newsletter published an article in support of Prop 8, illustrating in Kassidy's mind that there was an underlying assumption that if there was such a thing as a "Christian political agenda," this was it. But Kassidy wondered why Christians were so fired up and ready to stand up over this issue when they sat down for so many others issues like care for widows and orphans, justice for the poor and oppressed, hospitality to foreigners and immigrants. What was it about this issue and not the others that caused his church to move to action?

While wrestling with this issue and wondering what his response as a Christian should be, Kassidy found an online article about the issue that he understood to be provocative enough to generate honest and open conversation with those he trusted. He knew that many of his closest Christian friends would disagree with the position the author was advocating, but he posted it to MySpace in hopes that a genuine conversation would emerge and that such conversation would move Christians a little closer to understanding what a faithful response to such a challenging issue would entail. Those who disagreed with the article's position, Kassidy assumed, would have good reason, supported by thoughtful and prayerful opinions generated by the biblical, social, and theological implications that an article like this might bring to bear. But by Kassidy's recollection, none of these factors weighed into the responses he received. The comments that were left in response to the article haunt him to this day. "Friendships were lost," Kassidy shared. Instead of having a significant conversation, hateful words were blasted onto a message board, and people were hurt.

When it comes to the state of hospitable discourse in the church, politics is one area where Christians in the United States often fail with gusto. The extreme examples include picketing the funeral of a fallen American soldier, claiming that 9/11 was an act of divine judgment, or proclaiming that God stands ready to condemn rather than bless America. The tones of the conversations become discordant and often leave a young generation wondering if association with the church requires adopting a specific brand of politics that, in their ears, doesn't ring true to Christ's gospel.

In Kassidy's story, and many stories like his, political discourse tends to play a role in young people wondering whether or not there is a place for them in the church. Certainly the issues are a significant factor, but the kind of discourse itself is what leaves some wondering if they have a place in the conversation at all. In what we've seen in Kassidy's story, political discourse in the church becomes a liability to young people when their views are presumed by others to be aimed at unfaithful interpretations of Christ's gospel. Because young people are often statistically more likely to hold different political opinions than the generations in front of them, the discourse surrounding their opinions often leaves them wondering if their views are compatible with the gospel of Christ.

Surprisingly, while Protestant Christians are likely to attend a church in which most members are politically homogeneous, they don't want their churches to be overtly politicized. Opposition to political mobilization within churches runs deep across the board: eighty percent of Catholics, eighty-five percent of mainline Protestants, seventy-six percent of Black Protestants, and seventy-seven percent of Jews oppose their faith communities engaging in political action. "Most people come to church to hear about God, not Caesar."[1]

Yet even with this resistance to overt politicizing in our churches, there is a deep division among faith and politics. We live in a day and age when, more than any other time in the history of the United States, there is a strong and significant correlation between religious and political affiliation. People of faith, especially Evangelicals, Protestants, and Mormons, are the most likely to be affiliated and active with the Republican Party and conservative political opinions. While younger generations, ours included, might assume that's how it's always been, this just isn't the case. Prior to the social revolution of the 1960s, there was a statistically insignificant correlation between religion and politics. But for those born after 1982, we remember an

America where political conversation is charged with heated religious overtones.

Even though Christians don't want their pastors politicking from the pulpit, that doesn't mean they don't expect their churches to share their political values. For those of us who were born into this religious/political climate, we see an increasing skepticism about an assumed correlation between our religious and political identity.

Younger Christians are especially skeptical and less likely to be politically homogeneous. While they tend to be more conservative than their parents' generation on issues like abortion, they tend to be more liberal on issues like same-sex unions, but again, not homogeneous. Beyond these two hot-button issues, younger Christians find a variety of voices on issues like war, global trade policy, and poverty programs.

MANY YOUNGER CHRISTIANS FEEL THAT THEIR POLITICAL VIEWS AND EVEN THEIR PASSIONS ARE MET WITH A LESS-THAN-HOSPITABLE RECEPTION IN THEIR CHURCHES.

Because there is a generation of Christians who find themselves on the other side of this seismic political shift, skeptical of the politics of their parents' generation, it's not hard to see why many younger Christians feel that their political views and even their passions are met with a less-than-hospitable reception in their churches. Kassidy is one of many Christians who brought questions to the relationship between faith and politics and ended up fearful of having a conversation with other Christians about these issues. When our speech doesn't embody our faith in love and truth, even as we try to articulate it, silence wins the day, and silence cannot engender the kind of prophetic presence that is needed in our congregations to stir us toward more faithful representation of Christ's kingdom.

But didn't our mothers teach us not to discuss religion or politics at the dinner table? How can our generation engage in generous, hospitable conversations for the benefit of the Kingdom? Is there a place for young people in the church if they tend to associate with a different political party or differ in the way they think Christ's gospel should correspond to the political ordering of our society?

## I'M OKAY. YOU'RE OKAY?

All this talk about conversations may have you wondering if we are advocating an "anything-goes" theology in which whatever people do, think, or say is fine as long as they are open about it. While this may fit in well with the larger culture, this could not be farther from what we are trying to suggest.

Tune into almost any television show or movie with a primary audience between the ages of five and eighteen, and you will hear one very consistent theme: "I'm okay. You're okay. We're all okay just as we are. Nothing needs to change." It's a tune we hardly notice anymore, because it's like background noise, always there, filling the silence. The problem with this culturally pervasive mantra is that it simply isn't Christian. You don't have to look very far into Genesis to learn that we humans, while created good by a good God, are not okay as we are. Our good image hasn't been completely destroyed, but it is a bit twisted and confused. We are born as sinners, fallen from God's good and perfect design. Maybe it's been a while since you've cracked Genesis, but you don't have to look very far past the end of your nose to see the evidence of sin in the world. It is only by God's grace and the faithfulness of Jesus Christ, crucified and resurrected, that we are made whole, that the good image can be untangled. Thank God, we are forgiven just as we are, but we are certainly not okay. There is a lifetime of transformation waiting for us once we've accepted the redeeming work of Christ into our lives.

One Christian theologian named Augustine knew this all too well. From an early age Augustine knew that he had lots of desires for lots of things and that those desires were not bad in and of themselves but that because the divine image had been distorted, those desires led him to do distorted things. One night, when he was a young man, he and his friends saw a pear orchard belonging to a farmer, bearing fruit that was ready to go to market. Not knowing why exactly, he and his friends stole an armload of the fruit, using it to throw at pigs. Years later, he reflected back on why he would have stolen something from a farmer for such a senseless purpose and came to a general conclusion that his desire for food is not bad—only when that desire is misplaced, when it is not God-oriented. He went on to imagine a life in which all our desires are God-oriented and how transformative such a life could be.[2] Finally, in one of his most famous phrases, he confessed to his Maker, "You have made us for yourself, and our heart is restless until it rests in you."[3] In other words, our desires are incredibly powerful, which isn't a bad thing until they come uncoupled from a God-ward purpose.

In Augustine's vision, our desire for food should be aimed at health rather than gluttony, our desire for money should be aimed at well-being rather than greed, our desire for sex should be for our spouse rather than for adultery, and so on. Left to our own devices, however, our desires begin to carry us toward brokenness and pain. When that happens, Augustine saw the twisted image of the divine becomes all that we live by, and things start to get messy and broken. Augustine knew that not every desire we have is necessarily good just because we have that desire. For the sake of our own well-being, we should love and appreciate the desires God has given us, and then we need to ask if our actions based on those desires are God-oriented or not. Augustine helps us to see that too often our good desires become oriented toward other things and that this is when the divine image becomes most distorted and we are anything but okay.

So why do we keep buying the lie that we're all okay just as we are? In a word, *Glee*.

I'll be the first to confess, I tuned in week after week in the first season as this award-winning musical comedy-drama took the networks by storm in the fall of 2009. (Tim would like readers to know that it is Shawna writing here.) As somewhat of a musical theater geek myself, I couldn't resist the catchy tunes, seemingly spontaneous choreography, attractive young faces, and predictable yet addictive love triangles. If you can look past the atrocities committed to some of your favorite classic songs, you'll see that at its core, *Glee* is a modern underdog story.

The show follows one high school glee club as they travel the show choir circuit and deal with issues of self-image, sex, divorce, and friendship. Traditionally, the glee club was occupied by nerds who know all too well the victimization brought upon social underlings by football players and cheerleaders filling out their stereotypes, which usually involves pouring a slushy over the face of an underdog during passing periods. Laughing in the face of social stratus, this glee club is learning to re-write the stereotypes as they find their voices and challenge the status quo. Truthfully, though, the whole show is status quo.

Every episode teaches the viewer that he or she alone can know who he or she really is and that no one else can question that self-expression. Every desire you have is unquestioned, because it's an expression of an "inner you" that could never be critiqued. You create yourself. Every desire you have is good and makes you who you are. This is the status quo of modernity that upholds individuality above all else and places persons into nonjudgmental spheres in which no one and nothing can lay claim to their lives, challenge their behaviors, or, in the unforgivable assault on modernity, limit their self-expression.

In chapter 2 we referred to this as a brand of faith called moralistic therapeutic deism, a kind of theological structure in which God remains distant and uninvolved, so it is up to each person to create himself or herself. Religion is there to make you feel good about yourself but never to ask anything of you, and certainly not to suggest that anything is in need of transformation, redemption, or healing. In this approach to faith, every desire one has is simply a part of the "inner you" and therefore completely valid and good.

Back to Genesis: Christians know that we didn't and don't create ourselves. We were made in God's image and are being renewed in that image though Christ. Genesis reminds us that we are not made for self-expression but for divine expression. In fact, the word in Hebrew that we translate as *image* is actually a political word that was used to describe the statues that ancient kings would build in their outlying territories. When a king's army conquered a new territory, the people who lived in the territory often had never seen their new ruler, so the king would install an image of himself in that area to remind residents of who the new king was. In the same way, humans have been created in God's image, so when the world sees us, they immediately remember the king. That is, of course, when the image is restored and clear, free from sin and distortion.

We believe strongly in the power of God's grace to heal, to transform, and to be so present in our lives that it can actually reshape and transform our very desires, directing them in a God-ward orientation. In chapter 3 we talked about this in terms of the restoration of our identity in Christ's identity, something that John Wesley called holiness. We have the same idea in mind here, especially when it comes to being transformed into God's image, the image that originally marked us as humans and marks us again, reminding others of the image of our King.

We love it when Paul writes to the Christians in Corinth about seeing an image dimly reflected in a mirror. "Now we see only a reflection as in a mirror," he writes, "then we shall see face to face. Now I know in part; then I shall know fully, even as I am fully known" (1 Corinthians 13:12). Like a foggy mirror right after a shower, you can't see the image fully—you can see only, in part, a hazy image of what's really there. We don't really know who we are. We can't. The image in which we were created has been too blurred. It's only by looking to God and allowing God's grace to invade every part of our lives that we can know who we truly are: sons and daughters created in the divine image. Only when we are known by God can we know who we are.

But living in this divine image in a world that tells us we choose our own image seems nearly impossible at times. Cue the Church.

As we have already said, the Church is the sign and symbol of the kingdom of God in the world. God's kingdom isn't fully here just yet, but we are called to participate in it as a witness to the world around us, to be the image of the King. Our life together buffs up that image. Even though *Glee* tells us we are fine just as we are, the Church reminds us that we are not fully there just yet and that the image of God can be seen clearly only when God has healed and redeemed a people.

## HOLY CONVERSATIONS

So what does any of this have to do with young people and discourse about difficult issues? Basically, it means that the image of God ought to be present in the way we talk with one another so that the world can see a clear image of the King. Our churches are the places where Christians can talk together, can ask deep, hard questions, and can passionately disagree and sort through our pain and brokenness to discover God's truth. But if those things are to take place in and through conversation, such conversations must be holy conversations. They must be conversations that take place in the image of the King.

In our view, church ought to be where we are most real with one another. After all, it's assumed that if you're walking in that door, you may be a sinner, and you may or may not know it yet. So what is there to hide? It just makes sense that a church would be the place where the most genuine and authentic conversations can take place, the kind of conversations in which participants walk away reflecting a clearer image of God than when they walk in.

From what we've heard in Kassidy's story, we hope that our congregations can be places where we can share deeply and honestly and be real with one another. In his story, we saw a glimpse of the church as a hospitable place that made room for him to experience the redemptive power of Christ's grace, even in the face of disappointment and embarrassment. Yet so many people, especially those on the younger side of this cultural shift, feel that churches are the last place where they can be real about their struggles and questions, or, in David Kinnaman's words, "A generation of young Christians believes that the churches in which they were raised are not safe and hospitable places to express doubts."[4]

Perhaps you're frustrated that your congregation is not always that kind of a hospitable space. If that's you, ask honestly if you have bought into the *Glee* mantra. Do you assume that only you create your identity and that no one else can tell you who you are? Have you stopped listening for the truth that other people, even older people, have to speak into your life?

We certainly don't assume that every word spoken by anyone in your church is helpful, hospitable, or even true. Again, may we remind you, we were sinners who have been saved by grace. But we do hope that you haven't stopped listening for truth, even when it calls your life choices and behaviors into question.

When Kassidy told a man he respected that he had considered leaving his church to find a church where he would be fed, he was told, "You want to be fed? Go to the fridge." He went to his former youth pastor, who was now pastoring another church, to ask about looking for a new church, to which his former youth pastor said, "You want to look for a new church? That's fine, but don't come to mine. You're looking to relive something, and you won't find that here."

Kassidy was honest with two men he really respected and was faced with some hard truths. They didn't tell him what he wanted to hear and affirm that his desires were right on track no matter what they were. He was looking for an excuse to get out and go somewhere that would better serve his needs, not where he could truly serve the needs of others. Seeking out these two men and entering into holy conversation in which Kassidy was willing to hold up the mirror and question his perception of himself and his needs was the first step to finding his place in the Body of Christ.

Perhaps, however, you are on the other side of the sociological shift and wondering how your church can be a place that makes space for young people, especially when their political opinions appear disagreeable. If that's where you find yourself, we would suggest some holy conversation. You may not agree with the opinions that young people hold, they may appear confusing or even antithetical to the Christian faith you've come to know, but it's at that point that we would ask you to trust God and earnestly seek to engage a young person in the conviction that God will not lead you into untruth, but that as each of you is able to draw closer to God, the image of God can be even more clearly reflected in your relationship. Those are the kinds of conversations that are holy.

Today Kassidy admits that had he left the church in the midst of his struggles to find a place there, he can't imagine how he and Jenn would have coped with those first difficult years of marriage with a new baby. God used those conversation partners for a much bigger work of grace than Kassidy could have anticipated.

## CULTURE OF FEAR

Learning to have hospitable and holy conversations in the church begins with being a good conversation partner. Start by adopting a willingness to really listen and be challenged by others, even others who are genuinely dissimilar from you.

Admittedly, even if we are willing to listen and be challenged, we don't always find hospitable conversation partners. We live in an increasingly polarized society: we often know what we *don't* believe more strongly than what we *do* believe. Social scientists are coming to the conclusion that the climate of polarization is reaching new heights these days. Nolan McCarty, Keith Poole, and Howard Rosenthal, social scientists who have written *Polarized America: The Dance of Ideology and Unequal Riches*, argue that the massive social and economic changes of the last decade, most noticeably income disparity and immigration, have given way to an expansive divide in ideologies. More than in past decades, we find ourselves not just disagreeing with the bumper sticker on the car in front of us—but offended and enraged.[5]

The reason polarization plays into our discussion about conversation is simply because the farther away your conversation partner seems to be ideologically, the easier it is to either disengage or ratchet up your rhetoric to a roar. And once we are roaring, we aren't listening.

Shortly after the 2008 presidential election, we decided to give up cable television. Primarily, we gave it up because we were poor grad students and the free trial period was up. Also, these were the days when Netflix was offering streaming and rentals for one low price, about a third the cost of cable—days we sorely miss! But what finally pushed the button on the decision was the maddening effect of the twenty-four-hour news networks. FOX, MSNBC, even CNN jumped in the fray, all trying to say or report the more inflammatory story to gain a boost in ratings. Politicians we once respected sold out once-rational and cooperative views to the national hunger for blood and gore. We became so frustrated at what we were seeing that we found ourselves yelling back at the television set, no different from the foaming commentators who had first incited our rage.

The blood thirst isn't limited to the political arena. In recent years we've seen a dramatic increase in theological blogs, videos, articles, using heated, polarized, and sometimes hateful language to describe fellow Christians. Of course, as the degree of polarization increases, the scope of what people consider true or fundamental Christianity shrinks accordingly. In the same way that the political world was caught in a debate over who was in and who was out of the "real America," Christians seemed to be caught up in debating who was in and who was out of God's grace.

The debates rage on in the blogosphere where some will charge that postmodernity, and therefore any theology that attempts to function in light of a postmodern culture, is satanic in its origins and holds a worldview that even Satan himself holds. Where can the conversation possibly go from there? On what grounds could this author enter a conversation with someone who has found some postmodern precepts to be helpful for his or her faith and expect that discussion to result in mutual growth and discipleship? How can such rhetoric contribute to refining our image of the God who took on flesh and humbled himself to death on a cross?

We are not trying to make an argument for postmodern theology or modern theology or any other particular philosophical paradigm. Again, we think the gospel of Christ is bigger than any particular philosophical paradigm and that it cannot be perfectly crystallized in one or the other. Like many others, we feel that philosophies and worldviews come and go. None are inherently Christian, and yet like missionaries, we are called to live and witness in the culture and context in which God has placed us. We are not concerned with convincing you that postmodernity is good, bad, or indifferent. We are concerned, however, with the culture of fear and suspicion that results from a polarized climate impacting many churches and Christians, which has in turn led many young people to question whether or not they even have a home in the church.

Kassidy, who is a pretty outspoken individual, admitted that there are many times in his church and in conversations with friends when he just keeps his mouth shut, afraid that disagreeing or asking questions might trigger an explosive conversation that would result in damaged relationships. And we see hope in that, because we see that Kassidy is modeling for us a way of engaging the church, of being present, and of finding a place—through participating in significant and holy conversation by listening first.

If our churches are to be the places that welcome young people who wonder if they have a place, they must be real spaces of authentic, holy conversation. That doesn't mean we will never disagree, but it means that as we seek God's truth together, we trust deeply that the Spirit will not lead us away from goodness if we are truly open to God's transformative grace that redeems, transforms, heals, and orients our desires toward God. Too often we disagree with one another out of fear, confusion, and suspicion, leading some to believe that they don't have a place at the table. If we were to place our trust in God, however, and trust that the Holy Spirit is present and active in the Church, our conversations with one another need not be marked by fear and suspicion but by the hopeful, silent, and surprising ways that God is still using the Church for redemptive purposes in the world.

## RESTORED IMAGE

If our churches are going to better image the God who made us and heals us, we have to learn to be honest with each other, speaking the truth but speaking in fierce, unyielding love. This is the kind of love that begins with listening, offering the hospitable option that while another person may hold different opinions, his or her opinions are based in a desire for faithfulness. Of course, this requires both humility and just a little more common sense.

Humility is essential for conversation to be fruitful, because it means that each member is not so convinced of his or her own argument that the member closes himself or herself off to correction. Jesus modeled this for us in His conversation with the Syrophencian woman recorded in Matthew 15. Being fully God, Jesus already had a perfect love for her and a perfectly loving end in mind for that encounter. But He was also a Jewish man in the ancient world, surrounded by other Jewish men, who were all watching and waiting for His response. Jesus engaged this woman in genuine conversation, and His love for this woman allowed Him to be moved by her great faith and to tear down yet another social barrier. The position Jesus originally articulated was very much the correct position. God had sent Jesus to restore Israel, and this Gentile woman was an outsider with an unsavory opinion that didn't match the officially sanctioned view of the day. But in hearing what she had to say and engaging her in holy conversation, Jesus not only saw her faith but also gave her a place at the table.

Was Jesus right in His first words of rebuke to her? Was He advocating the correct idea? We are often tempted to quickly form an opinion about whether Jesus' rebuke was right or not. But in doing so, we've missed the point. Regardless of whether or not Jesus was right to begin with, His openness to authentic conversation opened a possibility for the woman to find a seat at the table and receive God's transformative and healing mercy, an option that would not have been open to her had Jesus been so convinced of His own position that He was unwilling to truly listen to the woman. No wonder Paul writes that Christ did not consider equality with God a thing to be grasped (Philippians 2). Christ's humility, especially in Matthew 15, is the very image of His divinity.

If this polarization, or culture of fear, or perhaps a simple lack of conversation partners is making it hard to find a seat at the table in your church, we would challenge you to ask God to make you into the kind of conversation partner you would like to encounter. Be open to the work of the Holy Spirit in your life, transforming you into the image of a humble king. Changing churches or checking out won't cure your spiritual frustration any more than giving up cable television could make us more caring, compassionate, or sane people. Only the Holy Spirit can do work like that.

Modeling humility in the midst of a divisive and polarized culture is exactly the kind of prophetic presence we are advocating. Not only could this result in a deepening of your own spiritual formation—it can also lead to a healthy unrest in your church as your presence of meekness challenges the status quo.

Accomplishing both humility and speaking the truth in love is a challenge, and it requires a degree of common sense. Social media can be a great place to engage with others in your congregation or Christians around the world. But on-line dialogue can also lead us to say and write things we would never say to someone face to face. Kassidy was shocked at the response to the article he posted on his MySpace page, an article with which he may or may not have even agreed. Ask yourself if Facebook, Twitter, or Blogspot is really the best place to have a meaningful conversation about the faith questions on your mind.

Also, don't underestimate the power of sitting down and sharing an actual meal with people, even people who are really different from you. The simple practices of hospitality—opening your home, eating together, pulling out a chair—often give way to hospitality of the heart and more generous attitudes.

## GETTING IN THERE AND FIXING IT

Kassidy's story is one that gives us hope, but it's also one that carries hope on the back of a challenge. In what we've seen in his story, Kassidy didn't step back and demand that others pull back a chair and offer him a seat at the table, but he accepted the challenge issued by someone of another generation to step up and engage, to be a prophetic presence, calling the church to greater faithfulness to God's mission in the world. There was also the challenge of authentic conversation, which sometimes includes allowing others in your church to make a claim upon your desires and actions and to call you to greater faithfulness to Christ's gospel. Ultimately, Kassidy found that the rewards for accepting these challenges were far beyond anything that a skeptical young man could have envisioned.

Accepting the challenge to engage, listen, and be a patient but prophetic presence in your congregation by speaking the truth in love may sound impossible, but where the Church is, there is the Spirit. Trust that God's Spirit is at work in your life and in your church. Commit to your own spiritual formation before complaining about the culture of your congregation. Ask God to change you first, to be the source of hospitality you are longing for in your church in the hopes that you will find a deeper welcome in the fellowship at your church. Engage those with whom you may disagree, even on tricky things like politics, and trust that the Spirit is at work in bringing both of you into deeper communion through the Spirit. And even if they are members of the Tea Party and you are a left-wing liberal, know that the authentic community found in the church will always be a tea party for two.

# SHRIMP CEVICHE 6 AT MIDNIGHT

**WE HAD NOT** encountered six-way intersections until we made our first trip through the city of Chicago. Situated along Lake Michigan, Chicago is a marvel of civil engineering, incorporating both grid-style east-to-west streets along with diagonal avenues that run into and away from the central part of downtown like spokes of a wheel.

Having driven from Kansas City that night, we were tired and a bit overwhelmed by the prospect of navigating a new city, let alone a city that had streets running every which way. At many Chicago intersections, you don't simply turn right or left, because there are two right options and two left options. That's probably why we got as lost as we did in trying to find Edward and Liz's house.

A few weeks earlier, we had made the hard decision to leave the community of friends we had come to love in Kansas City so that Tim could pursue further education, and with that came new possibilities for ministry. I (Shawna) had turned to the Internet and began reaching out to contacts in and around Chicago, looking for openings in churches and other ministry sites that would want a recent seminary grad who was willing to take on a new assignment so that her husband could complete a graduate degree. When I contacted Edward, he said that not only would he be willing to help us but that we should stay at his home when we came to Chicago to explore the possibilities. We had met Edward and Liz in Kansas City several months earlier when he was completing his seminary studies through a distance-learning program. Edward was a Chicago native who knew the city intimately and was capable of navigating six-way intersections with ease.

When we were finally able to find the house, it was well after midnight, and there wasn't any evidence of anyone inside being awake. Edward quietly appeared at the door, though, and escorted us into the two-story classic home and to our room, which was located on the bottom floor just off the kitchen. Deeply tired, we went about our bedtime routine as quickly as possible, hoping for a few hours of much-needed rest.

It was the sounds of life, rather than the light of day, that woke us up the next morning. Children were playing and laughing as dishes were clinking together, the reverberations of a family making itself ready for the day. Based on what we heard from the kitchen, we weren't sure what to expect when we opened the door of the guest room. As we think back on it, we suppose that only those who have ever received a completely undeserved and gratuitous welcome can really understand what we experienced that morning. If you've had that kind of welcome before, you know that it's sweetly surprising, and a little fierce in the way that it disarms your anxiety of meeting new people and experiencing a new place so quickly. As we hastily learned, Edward's brother and his family occupied the lower level of the large dwelling, and it was their kitchen in which we were now standing. They greeted us warmly as we introduced ourselves to them, though they were dressed and ready for the day and we still bore the disheveled appearance of weary travelers.

After breakfast Edward took us on a driving tour of Chicago, seemingly leaving no neighborhood unexplained. He drove patiently through the bustling streets, explaining the economic, ethnic, and sociological dynamics that have shaped the city's seventy-seven distinct neighborhoods and talking about the way the various churches have attempted to engage the city. Our tour concluded that evening just after sunset when Edward turned up Lake Shore Drive and exited for the Adler Planetarium, driving us onto the long peninsula that affords the most spectacular views of the Chicago skyline. We marveled at the city, of course, but even more at Edward's willingness to take an entire day to introduce two young travelers to the city he loved so deeply.

We made the drive back through Chicago to his house, where we shared an incredible dinner of traditional Guatemalan food that Liz had prepared. It was getting late as were making our way downstairs when we saw there was a light on in the kitchen, where Edward's brother, sister-in-law, and another guest were sharing a large bowl of something that we had never seen before but immediately knew we would like.

"What is it?" we asked as our hosts passed a bag of tortilla chips to us to scoop up the delicious fusion of avocado, tomato, shrimp, and other things.

"Shrimp ceviche," said Liz as she smiled. "It's one of our favorites, and we thought you might like it."

She was right. Together, our small group finished off most of the contents of the bowl as we laughed and talked late into the night.

It was precisely this kind of welcome that came to our minds as we began pondering what a hospitable welcome might mean for those who are wondering if they have a place in the church. Being in a new city with new people and a new culture are often the times when one feels the most like an outsider, as if he or she doesn't have a place at the table. Why, then, did we feel so welcome with our new friends that night? What was it about our encounter with them that opened up possibilities for relationship that would not have been present in the absence of their hospitality? We knew that in thinking hopefully about the place of a generation who seeks a place at the church's table, we needed to tell Edward's story.

## SOCCER OR BASKETBALL?

"I was a complete stranger," Edward told us as he reflected on his experience relating to the church. "My whole family was made up of strangers in a new land because of our immigrant background."

At home, Edward's family spoke Spanish, but outside of his house, Edward began to distance himself from his family's heritage. "In those days," he told us, "only the strong would survive, and that meant one had to melt into the larger culture to achieve the ideal of becoming North American.

Being from an unchurched family also contributed to Edward's sense of being a stranger as he tried to relate to the church. "We weren't an atheist family," he told us. "We had reverence for God, but we weren't accountable to a faith community, which meant that we were just unfamiliar with the church." As a young man, Edward's encounters with the church were sporadic and usually associated with holidays like Christmas and Easter. The church simply wasn't a familiar place for him, so he didn't feel he had a real place there.

EDWARD FOUND THAT THE CHURCH COMMUNITY WAS A PLACE OF SURPRISING SUPPORT AND RESOURCE FOR A YOUNG MAN WHO DIDN'T ALWAYS FEEL AT HOME IN HIS SURROUNDINGS.

He did know that he had a place, however, among his friends at school. "It was friendship in those natural spaces," he said, that began to open a sense of being familiar with the church. His friends at school were Christians, but they were also Hispanic and shared a common background with Edward in that they were strangers in a new land together. "When I finally came to a church service for the first time," Edward recollected, "it wasn't like I was a complete oddball. There was definitely a sense of being new, but I knew people there, and that was good. It was gradual—like any relationship."

Edward's relationship with the church grew stronger. He found that the church community was a place of surprising support and resource for a young man who didn't always feel at home in his surroundings. "As a teenager," he said, "I didn't look at the church with the typical attitude of 'Why bother?' because it was a place that very unexpectedly broadened my horizons. The people there believed in me, and they supported me in my dreams."

Granted, Edward's church was not a community of unlimited resources. They were an immigrant population, strangers traveling together in a strange new land. Many of the people in his congregation didn't have the chance to earn much more than a sixth-grade education, but they encouraged Edward to push past the barriers that often stand in the way of education when a family is simply trying to establish themselves in a new place. "They were so joyful of my endeavors," he told us, speaking about educational opportunities. "Not all of them did it themselves, but they saw something in me, and they encouraged me toward it."

Generational dynamics were always a part of his experience in the church, Edward told us, but his story bears a distinctive sense of engagement in the midst of those generational differences. When we worshiped at his church with him during our visit to Chicago, we experienced an incredibly vibrant multigenerational service. Babies were dedicated while grandparents and great-grandparents happily observed. The sermon that morning was probably the best Spanish lesson either one of us had received in quite a while, and we listened to scriptural points illustrated by references to Diego Maradona, an Argentine soccer star.

It's there, Edward told us after the service, that the generational divide begins to emerge. "These kids were born in Chicago," he said, motioning to a large group of high school students. "They don't know who Diego Maradona is, or if they do, they probably don't care as much as their parents—they know about Derrick Rose," he said, referring to the NBA guard signed to the Chicago Bulls.

In Edward's context, the young generation could very much seem placeless in the church. The generational divide in his congregation wasn't marked by adherence to a particular worldview or philosophical outlook but by cultural identification. For those in his church who had come to Chicago as adults, their cultural identification was with their country of birth, yet their own children identified with a different country of birth. Like Edward, they, too, struggled with a sense of distance from their family's heritage, often wondering if opportunity and success would require them to turn away from their own families.

Yet the church was brimming with youth. High school students, college students, and young professionals were present in incredible percentages, many of whom were integrated into the life of the church, serving throughout the service, all seeming thrilled to be at church.

We couldn't help but wonder what could make the difference for so many young people in finding a seat at the table. "Relationships are very fluid in the Hispanic community," Edward explained. "Even in house gatherings, there is a strong sense of connection, and that sense takes precedence over other generational dynamics. Even though these generations do things differently, those relationships far outweigh the importance of our differences."

It's that strong sense of the importance of relationships that runs throughout Edward's story and has shaped his ability to find a place in the church as a young man. "I had a good relationship with the older crowd," he told us about his early days in the church. "But I also had a good relationship with the younger crowd. It can be so easy to create dualisms," he continued. "You find people who are on different sides of an issue, and they're arguing their points, thinking that they're convincing the other side of their point, when all they're actually doing is creating dualisms."

The dualisms Edward talks about are those that have deeply marked our society and have significantly contributed to the so-called generational divide we've explored in earlier chapters. But in his understanding, Edward sees that a strong sense of cross-generational relationship opens up hospitable space for generations to be drawn together rather than being defined by points of disagreement. And that space, he tells us, is a space in which young people can find a place in the church.

When Edward was preparing to graduate from high school and considering the possibilities of his future, the United States military appeared to him to be an avenue of further experience and education. Enlisting in the Marines, Edward experienced a difficult period of life in which he would come to discover what his faith would look like in a completely different context. "The things I was required to learn, the things I was required to train to do, and the things I actually had to do," he said, "were a complete contrast to the peacemaking nature of the church." He told us it was his time in the military that began to strengthen his tendencies toward peacemaking and his instincts to approach difficult situations by locating points of similarity rather than difference. It's also that peacemaking instinct that we see as a hopeful aspect of the church's ability to make a place at the table for young people who wonder if they are simply too different to be offered a space.

Peacemaking, according to Edward, doesn't mean there will be a complete absence of tension in a congregation, but it does mean we will approach difficult conversations with a goal of togetherness rather than domination of the opposition. "Look at our society today," Edward said. "Everyone wants to show how different they are from other people. They want to use their differences to define themselves, and that just leads to more dualisms and distance between people." As he spoke, he went on to refer to Moody Bible College, just blocks away from where Edward works as part of his ministry in Chicago. "We have differences in our approach to the Christian faith, yes," he acknowledged, "but I'm not going to begin with those differences when I talk to someone from Moody. I'm a Wesleyan, but that doesn't mean I need to create a dualism with someone who approaches Christianity differently. In every scenario there will be difference, but we need to see what will draw us closer."

> PEACEMAKING, ACCORDING TO EDWARD, DOESN'T MEAN THERE WILL BE A COMPLETE ABSENCE OF TENSION IN A CONGREGATION, BUT IT DOES MEAN WE WILL APPROACH DIFFICULT CONVERSATIONS WITH A GOAL OF TOGETHERNESS RATHER THAN DOMINATION OF THE OPPOSITION.

## DEALING WITH DUALISM

We think Edward's story is one that can open a lot of exciting possibilities when it comes to helping young people find a place in the church. The vision of the church that we encounter in Edward's story is one that begins with relationality and the ability to live together in peace without allowing the differences between generations to degenerate into suspicion.

We are also particularly hopeful, however, about the way that Edward's experience draws attention to the way we North American Christians tend to see the world in terms of dualisms and the tension that such a view often places on seeing the world in terms of relationships. Historically, dualism has been a way the church has tended to operate theologically in the modern era. Dualistic thinking is neat, clean, and categorical, because it is often predisposed to take an idea, person, institution, and so on, and place it into an either-or framework. Perhaps the most well-known dualisms are those that distinguish between good and evil, faith and reason, religion and science, and so on. According to this dualistic way of thinking, each concept plays against the other in a kind of zero-sum balance, which means that if something is not completely good, then it must be completely bad.

Whether it's because we've inherited a dualistic way of thinking from ancient Greek philosophy, whether it's because our athletic games usually involve the pitting of one team against another, whether it's because the United States is governed by a two-party political system, or whether it's an issue of theological dualism, we often think in dualistic terms so that there must be an opposing response to nearly every statement made by another person.

Consider recent political discourse. Often people who hold different political ideologies have a hard time coming to agree with one another on just about anything, because we tend to think in zero-sum terms, knowing that if I possess the truth on an issue, there's no way the other person can at the same time. The idea here is that if I am *completely* right, then you are *completely* wrong. And we are often convinced that we *are* completely right.

There are at least a couple of problems with dualism for Christians, theologically speaking. First, we believe in a God who created the whole universe, not just what we understand to be the good parts. Second, we are a people who believe in a God who became flesh, a mind-bending confession that defies dualism in attempting to understand what took place in Jesus' incarnation.

Dualism was a tempting way to make sense of Jesus for early Christians who really struggled with how to make sense of how the man they saw, loved, and knew could be divine *and* human. In the first attempts to make sense of it, He was part God and part human. He was either-or. He was zero-sum. That led early theologians to make all kinds of creative proposals to help us understand what was going on with God becoming flesh in Jesus. One well-known suggestion was that His mind or His soul (they were one in the same concept for early

Christians) was divine but that His body was human and that when the disciples watched Jesus die on the Cross, it was His body that died, but His divine mind remained alive.

Again, the problem here was that dualistic thinking, neatly dividing up Jesus into "divine" and "human" categories, just didn't seem to be helpful. If Jesus' mind wasn't at all human, what are we to make of our minds? Is there any hope that our minds can be redeemed if Jesus never actually assumed a human mind? And even further still, if Jesus were divided up into these categories, what does that mean for *our* souls? Do we possess minds or souls that are something other than human?

Christians have almost always struggled with using a dualistic either-or to make sense of the world. In the dualism of body and soul, we tend to assume that certain aspects of life apply to one or the other. Food, for example, applies to the body, while prayer applies to the soul. Sex, again, is a body thing, while the soul deals with worship. And the whole schema is zero-sum, so everything must fall into one of those two categories.

It's not at all our purpose to dig deeply into the history or nature of dualistic thought, but we did want to give this brief exposition so that we can try to bring to light some hopeful theological reflection for those searching for a place in the church but have encountered a dualistic reality in the church. Especially in what we've heard in Edward's story, dualistic thinking has tended to be used as a wedge to discern between good and evil. The troubling aspect of this dynamic, however, is that it becomes very hard to approach life that way when we believe that the most truly human person ever to have lived, by His very nature, explodes the categories of dualism, bringing all of reality under His truth and goodness.

So what does any of this have to do with helping young people find a place in the church? In Edward's story, he highlighted the kinds of conversation that would take place between generations in the Church. At times, those conversations can be characterized by differences that emerge in the way the generations think and act and the ways in which they approach the Christian faith. If dualism is the way in which those interactions are approached, the result is that one partner in the conversation will be completely right while the other partner will be completely wrong. If this is the case, there is an immediate breach as one side no longer has a place among the faithful.

As we hear Edward's story and as we are challenged by the way he was able to find a place in the church as a young outsider, we recognize that our own lives haven't been immune to dualistic thinking and how harmful that has been to helping outsiders receive a welcome in the church. Both of us can remember times we were convinced that someone in the church had to be completely wrong, that their approach to Christianity was so outdated and irrelevant that it must be a completely wrong approach. May God forgive us for those times, and may the Holy Spirit redeem our thoughts.

So where is the hope? It is that the Christian biblical and theological tradition offers us a way of seeing reality that isn't dualistic. This tradition offers us the gift of being able to trust that the world is not an either/or kind of reality, but that as a God-created whole it is a reality that is unified under God's creative mercy, grace, and the hope of redemption. There are several ways this happens, and while we don't have room to go through all of these, we'll briefly mention a few.

## BIBLICAL BASIS

The writers of the Bible didn't assume that the world was dualistic. They didn't think of humans in dualistic terms or divide the soul from the body as we tend to do today. Instead, they saw humans as wholly unified beings: body, soul, mind—everything. We catch the first glimpse of this at the beginning of Genesis. "Now the earth was formless and empty," we find in Genesis 1:2, "darkness was over the surface of the deep, and the Spirit of God was hovering over the waters." The word we translate as *Spirit* is a Hebrew word, *ruach*, which is also translated as *breath* or *wind* in other parts of the Old Testament. One of those is in the very next chapter of Genesis. "Then the Lord God formed a man from the dust of the ground and breathed into his nostrils the breath of life, and the man became a living being" (Genesis 2:7). Notice the connection between life and *ruach* in this passage. Essentially, there is no life apart from the *ruach*. It is the presence of the *ruach* that gives life, that animates mere dust, that enters dirt and brings it to life.

This is what the biblical writers have in mind when they talk about the spirit's relationship to the body. It isn't necessarily that humans possess an eternal soul that gets beamed in at the beginning of life as much as it is that the spirit itself is what brings a person to life in wholeness. Many of the concepts we have about our body's relationship to our spirit (which we received more from Greek pagan philosophers than biblical sources) wouldn't make a lot of sense to the biblical writers. They wouldn't understand that a soul lives on without a body, because when God creates, it is the unity between body and soul that makes a human. We tend to think that our essence is in our souls and that our body doesn't particularly matter for that essence, but Genesis paints a different picture of human life being a unification of body and spirit. When the spirit departs or withdraws, unified, whole life is no longer possible.

We catch another glimpse of this in Genesis 8, just after the flood. God has just finished flooding the world; Noah, his family, and his animals are now treading water in the ark, waiting for the next step. "But God remembered Noah and all the wild animals and the livestock that were with him in the ark," we see in Genesis 8:1, "and he sent a wind over the earth, and the waters receded." There are echoes of Genesis 1 here as God's *ruach* hovered over the waters, bringing order to chaos. Now, the same *ruach* restores order to chaos, suggesting that when the *ruach* withdraws, chaos and death are the result.

Ezekiel's experience with the valley of dead bones gives us another hint. After Ezekiel watches in amazement as bones are knitted together with tendons and skin, he opens his mouth to speak the words God had given him to say to the newly formed bodies: "I will put my Spirit [*ruach*] in you and you will live" (Ezekiel 37:14).

Jesus, too, from the cross "breathed his last," according to Mark 15:37, while Matthew 27:50 prefers another description: "He gave up his spirit"—suggesting that both Mark and Matthew understood death to be a departure of spirit. Later, after His resurrection, Jesus breathed on His disciples and said, "Receive the Holy Spirit" (John

20:22), suggesting that the reception of the Spirit *(ruach)* is that which gives life.

All this is to say that the biblical writers didn't assume that the human life was a dualistic existence with a sharp distinction between body and soul. Instead, they saw human existence as the result of raw matter with God's life-giving *ruach*, which organizes, brings order from chaos, animates, and makes us whole. This is why Paul's description of the life to come is one of bodily resurrection rather than disembodied souls (1 Corinthians 15). John's vision of the world made right in Revelation, too, is a vision not of disembodied souls but of resurrected people whose bodies had been raised to life, even still bearing the marks of their martyrdom (Revelation 5:6). The biblical tradition simply sees a unity between body and spirit such that as soon as the body gives up its spirit, the being is returned to dust.

## GET INTO GOOD

Throughout the history of Christianity, many theologians have suggested that the most faithful way to understand good and evil is not through dualism but rather through understanding God as the Creator of all things. Thomas Aquinas, for example, wrote that evil does not exist in and of itself but that evil is simply the lack of goodness. A being, he goes on to say, is not evil because it shares in evil but because it fails to share in good and thus suffers a deprivation of goodness that we call evil. In the same way that darkness is only the absence of light, evil is simply the absence of goodness. Many theologians have followed his lead here and have suggested how helpful this can be for us.

Dualism, as we remember, would say that good exists and evil exists, and that everything is classified either as good or evil. Christian theology, however, suggests that good exists and that evil is simply a lack of goodness. Why does this matter? It matters because Christians orient themselves toward goodness rather than toward a dichotomy between good and evil. In other words, the Christian imagination sees God as the source of goodness and that all things that exist, by virtue of their existence, take part to some degree in God's goodness. When one turns away from that goodness, he or she turns toward destruction, toward sin and death, toward evil.

Aquinas argued that we ought to "get into" goodness as much as possible, to draw near to God. As we draw near to God, we are drawn toward life, wholeness, health, and away from evil, destruction, and chaos. But evil is simply the lack of goodness. Goodness is really what exists.

This approach, we think, opens up the possibility for Christians to engage the world with an incredible amount of hope, understanding that God's goodness extends to creation, or creation would no longer exist. And that, we think, can help us significantly in conversations with different generations, because we approach those conversations knowing that viewpoints that are different than ours are not cast in being necessarily all good or all evil, because to some degree both viewpoints participate in God's goodness. Granted, some viewpoints may participate a bit more fully in God's goodness, but at the very least, this approach gives us a way of approaching conversations beyond dualisms that set us entirely at odds with one another. Once we can trust in the goodness of reality, it opens the door for us to be less and less suspicious of viewpoints and opinions that differ from our own. As Edward said, dualism tends to increase the distance between people, rather than bring them together. Often dualism also has the sad consequence of maintaining that something is completely bad if it rubs up against whatever we think is good.

WE'VE BEEN CALLED TO CREATE PEACE," EDWARD SAID, "NOT MORE DUALISMS THAT LEAD TO DISTANCE BETWEEN PEOPLE."

For those who wonder if the church has a place for them at the table, we want to offer the hope that we hear in Edward's story, to commend to you the way that he doesn't see the church in terms of dualism but in terms of a whole reality, a kind of family that may have different ways of doing things such as worshiping, praying, preaching, learning, but to seek the ways in which these ways are neither completely good nor completely evil. When we slip into dualisms like that, we often find ourselves setting ourselves against another person or group in the church along the strictest lines, and this often results in someone without a place at the table, wondering if he or she will need to be sustained on the crumbs that fall. "We've been called to create peace," Edward said, "not more dualisms that lead to distance between people." We couldn't agree more.

## COMMITMENT AND ENGAGEMENT

Edward's story has been a challenging reminder to us to engage the church, and to do so in such a way that we do not set up dualisms. It is a challenging reminder to us that when we are seeking a place in the church, there is often a requirement on our part to lay down the pride of our complete correctness and find points of commonality with those who sit at the table alongside us.

Does this mean it will take some work and commitment to find a place? Yes, it does. Every relationship requires some amount of effort. But Edward's story stands as a grace-filled reminder to us that receiving a welcome requires engagement. Consider the Gentile woman in Matthew 15 who came to engage and was ultimately surprised by the kind of welcome she received. Edward, too, was surprised at the welcome he found in the church—but only once he engaged the community.

It was a fascinating dynamic that we asked Edward about. We wanted to know how he dealt with the tension between asking for a welcome and receiving a welcome and what role commitment might play in that. Or, in other words, why bother engaging the church for a place if it requires something of us? Why bother seeking out a place there if it isn't convenient?

"I find it a bit strange that we make our decisions based on convenience," he told us, going on to suggest that there are rarely other situations in life that allow us to meaningfully engage on the basis of convenience alone. "There are always inconvenient moments in my own home," he said, "but that doesn't mean I stop being committed to my wife and to my family."

In listening to his descriptions of engaging the church, we couldn't help but notice Edward's inclination to associate his significant relationship with the church with his significant relationship with his family. This association suggests to us that Edward's ability to engage the church has something to do with a long-term outlook when it comes to the church. He takes his relationships seriously, and that leads him to make commitments beyond convenience.

In much of the literature on young people and the church, there seems to be a correlation between convenience and church commitment. Because the younger generation tends to be less inclined than their grandparents to make commitments to institutions, there is an assumption that they will not commit to the church unless the church makes commitment easy. That kind of idea, though, seems to us to offer little hope and leaves us wondering why the church is worth a commitment if it requires so little. The hope we see in Edward's story is that he understands the value of deep commitment and that such commitment leads to surprising gifts that he would not have received otherwise.

What is interesting about Edward's story, though, is his use of the familial language to describe the nature of his commitment to the church. In other words, his commitment is not to an institution but to people. These deep relationships have arisen because Edward was willing to commit, was willing to take a vow, so to speak, and to let those relationships speak into his life in formative and significant ways. "The world is a place of brokenness," Edward told us when he was speaking about the nature of his commitment to relationships in the church. "Vows are being broken all the time. But that doesn't justify a world without commitment, a world without vows."

These commitments have claimed Edward, and he has submitted himself to the influence of the relationships they represent. It's not often you find a case being made for submission. Usually, if you're trying to help someone, you want him or her to be the "best self," or at least that's what we're told to do. This approach is actually rooted in a concept of ourselves that sees that there is nothing wrong, that we are in no need of change, and that every thought and desire we have is a legitimate one.

But that story can only carry you to the limits of your own abilities. In making commitments and submitting oneself to the authority of those relationships, we sense that there is a significant way in which we can find a seat at the table, exactly because tables are places of mutual hospitality. Imagine inviting someone to dinner but never submitting to the relationship that has been established, content with doing your own thing.

Not long ago, Tim was sitting in a train station in downtown Chicago doing some reading. Next to him were two men who appeared to be coworkers at a nearby construction site. They each brought their food to the table, sat down, and began eating their meal in complete silence, looking off into the distance as if the other weren't there at all. There was something extremely awkward about their behavior around a common table, and it was uncomfortable to watch. When thinking about Edward's story, the image of those men came to mind, because so many of us are tempted to find a seat at the table as those men found a seat at the table. We want to be totally unaffected by the other people at the table, but that's not the kind of community that can offer much in terms of transformation.

THE KIND OF TABLE WE HEAR ABOUT IN EDWARD'S STORY IS A TABLE OF PEOPLE SHARING, TALKING, LAUGHING, GIVING THEMSELVES TO THE SITUATION, SUBMITTING TO THE RELATIONSHIPS THAT ARE THERE, RATHER THAN HOLDING THEMSELVES AT A DISTANCE.

The kind of table we hear about in Edward's story is a table of people sharing, talking, laughing, giving themselves to the situation, submitting to the relationships that are there, rather than holding themselves at a distance. It's a table much like the one that was set in Edward's kitchen that night we felt so welcome. And as we gave ourselves to the formation that comes from the relationships, we were given the incredible gift of a hospitable welcome. We are still glad that we did. We are still glad that we sought to engage in meaningful relationship-building rather than sit in our room by ourselves. In engaging, in giving ourselves to the relationship, we made it possible for Edward and Liz to offer hospitality that night, and we found a place at their table.

A book aimed at helping young people find a place in the church will have some suggestions for the ways in which the church needs to change. If hospitality isn't being offered, often it's because you're dealing with a bad host, and you need to do something about the host. But Edward's story reminds us that in helping young people find a place in the church we also need to issue a challenge to young people to give themselves to significant and meaningful relationships, to commit to developing those relationships, and to find a surprising welcome in the process.

"I had a great relationship with the older generation," Edward said in remembering himself and his journey to find a welcome in the church. That willingness to commit to members of the older generation and to develop a relationship with them also gave him the ability to know that he didn't want to foster dualisms but to commit to finding common places of conversation and formative relationship. Looking past the dichotomy of dualism, Edward could recognize within an older generation their participation in goodness and their common ground in that goodness. His deep relational commitment opened a place to him to receive their welcome and to make a space for him at the table.

For those who are wondering if there is a place in the church, we want to offer a story that can out-narrate the story of individualistic self-sufficiency. We want to offer a story of submission to relationships, a story of committing to another and allowing him or her to speak formatively into your life. And we want to suggest that when you do so, you may receive a welcome that you had no idea was possible.

# PART 3

# PRACTICING WITH IMAGINATION

# DO
## 7 EYE
# NEED
# YOU?

**IN THE STORIES** we've told so far, we've been hinting at some ideas that we hope will make a real difference for those who are wondering if there is still a place for them in the church. But there's no getting away from it: the church is a theological entity. What we mean is that the church is far more than a group of people who have decided to get together for weekly social events and a motivational speech. It's far more than that. In fact, we would go so far as to say that the church is what God is doing to bring about the healing of the world today.

We know that's an awfully big claim, because how would God choose such a seemingly broken, backwards, and sometimes strange way to bring about healing and wholeness in this world? The amazing thing about the story of God's healing of the world is that God has a long track record of choosing strange ways of bringing about healing and redemption. And if you've been around the church for any amount of time, you've probably realized how strange it can be.

In what we're about to claim, "strange" isn't going to be something we're going to shy away from. In fact, we're going to embrace it. We're going to suggest that the church's strange and peculiar way of being itself is exactly what requires an opening of space for those who are wondering if there is room for them anymore. This chapter is going to be a bit different from the others, because we're going to get a bit theological again—there's no escaping it—but in a way we hope will be surprising and hopeful to those who are wondering if their seats at the table have been taken away.

WE SIMPLY WANT TO SUGGEST THAT THE KIND GOD WHO CALLS THE CHURCH INTO EXISTENCE OUGHT TO MATTER FOR THE WAY WE LIVE OUR LIFE TOGETHER AS THE CHURCH.

Here's where we're headed: We're going to take a few steps first before we dive into the good theology that we think will make a difference for the church today. Don't worry if you're not a philosophy genius or a profound theologian. We simply want to suggest that the kind God who calls the Church into existence ought to matter for the way we live our life together as the Church. We're going to take the first steps by narrating a story we think has led to some of the problems you may be sensing in the church today. Once we've done that, we'll talk through a theological doctrine that we hope will help, then finish out with a few chapters on what that might look like on a practical level.

## EYE DON'T NEED MY FOOT

Have you ever looked at a carton of milk and seen that whoever designed the label wanted to make a big deal out of the fact that it's been homogenized? As you probably remember from your science classes, homogenization is the process of taking a substance that might contain all kinds of different variations and making it all the same. It's a good thing for milk, because it kills off the bacteria that can cause the milk to go bad or cause certain kinds of infections in those who drink it.

But homogenization isn't a process we want to see the church go through. What might be good for milk is something that we think is really, really harmful for a strange entity like the Church. Homogenization is all about washing away distinctions; it's all about making everything the same and getting rid of anything that might be just a bit different. You might be getting where we're headed with this.

Homogenization is a wonderful and healthful thing for milk, but when it comes to the Church, it becomes problematic, because the Church is that unique body of believers that is made up of all tribes and nations. There may not be anyone who's done a better job on this issue than Paul as he wrote to the group of believers in Corinth just as the Church was beginning to come into existence—"If the whole body were an eye, where would the sense of hearing be?" he asks, likening the church to the human body. "If the whole body were an ear, where would the sense of smell be? But in fact God has placed the parts in the body, every one of them, just as he wanted them to be. If they were all one part, where would the body be? As it is, there are many parts, but one body" (1 Corinthians 12:17-20).

Paul does an incredible job here of holding together two ideas that are necessary to the Church's being: particularity and unity. On the one hand, he makes the strong claim that we can't all be exactly alike—we can't be homogenized. If we are, any kind of particularity is washed away; and just like a pile of livers isn't a body, neither is the Church that has attempted to wash away any kind of particularity.

When we look to those who are wondering if there is a place in the church for them, we often see hints of a tendency to homogenize, to curtail particularity, as if it isn't needed. We've seen friends and colleagues assume that they simply are no longer welcome in the Body of Christ because the church sometimes struggles with making space for particularity, like Rick, who wondered if he couldn't be a pastor because he didn't go to the same hair stylist as his pastor.

At the same time (and this is his genius), Paul makes sure that we understand that even in our particularity there is unity, namely the unity that comes from worshiping the God of Jesus Christ. In other words, the Church isn't just a collection of particular persons for no reason. Instead, the Church is that strange and unique body that God has called into being for His purposes for healing and redemption in the world. "There are different kinds of gifts, but the same Spirit distributes them," Paul reminds us. "There are different kinds of service, but the same Lord. There are different kinds of working, but in all of them and in everyone it is the same God at work" (1 Corinthians 12:4-6). It's God who unifies us, not that we don't need particularity, because we do. We assemble as particular persons but in the name of our Head.

The two key ingredients in Christian communion are submission to Christ's lordship and particularity. When these mix, Christian communion is the incredible result. As a way of getting at this concept, we hope you'll take a moment to endure a strange comparison.

What we've just described could be likened to a softball team. A softball team has a singular purpose and goal: to win softball games. But if everyone on the team were exactly the same, could they win? If a team is made up of all pitchers but has no outfielders, what are the chances of their success? What if every member of the team were infielders, but there were no batters? What we're after is the image that we need the differences in one another to be a community. That community unites around a singular mission or purpose—Jesus' lordship, in the case of the Church—but we would all be in trouble if we possessed exactly the same skills, backgrounds, or views of the softball field.

To push the comparison just a bit further, suppose the third baseman on the team sees the catcher preparing for a game by putting on her pads and face mask. The third baseman might assume that the catcher had no idea what she was doing and that she wasn't really a softball player because she obviously doesn't know how to dress the part. Every third baseman knows that softball players don't wear pads and a face mask! Or maybe the centerfielder watches a pitcher throw a softball. Every centerfielder knows that a softball is thrown overhand, but for some reason, it's an underhand throw seen here.

The differences between the players on the team could be a source of suspicion. Their particular ways of dressing for the game and their particular ways of throwing the ball could cause the other players on the team to think they really aren't softball players at all. But we all know that the softball team depends on the particularity of its players. If everyone dressed like the catcher or threw the ball like the pitcher, it's pretty likely the softball team would be miserable.

In the case of the softball team, they need two things: unity around a common mission (winning games) and differences among the players. The same is true for the Church. There is first unity around a common mission (the redemptive gospel of Jesus Christ), and then there is the particularity of each of the members. Both are necessary. Neither can be dismissed.

One of the things we continue seeing in churches today is getting the particularity right but the unity under Christ wrong, and suddenly, every cause that every member has becomes that thing that the church *must* do. In some churches, though, we've seen that those with well-meaning passion never stop to wonder if these desires are really unified with God's purposes of redemption and healing. All of this is to say there is a "both-and" to the life in the church: there is a necessary particularity, but at the same time, all of those particular people are assembled under one purpose, and that purpose, thank God, is not of our own invention. It's something bigger than us, something worth giving our lives for. We just want to be sure that if we are going to call the church to give itself for something, it's something we're joining God in doing rather than something we've invented ourselves.

You've heard us talk a bit about the *Glee* approach to life and how that can become problematic for not only finding a place in the church but also for living a whole life in God's image. When it comes to the "both-and" of particularity and unity, the *Glee* approach gets particularity but has a harder time grasping unity. In other words, we can demand that the church listen to our particularity—and with it we can insist that the church never questions our desires or intent. But that's not the vision of the church Paul had in mind, nor is it a church that would be very interesting. What makes the church fascinating, challenging, and transformative is that particularity is maintained *within and because of* the unity of submitting to Christ's lordship. Particularity on its own is not community. Homogenization is not community either. The church is that uniquely wonderful community that welcomes its members to live out their particularity in service and submission to Christ. No other kind of community can protect particularity in that way.

We're going to use one more ridiculous example for a moment to illustrate what we're talking about. Suppose a man comes to your local

WHAT MAKES THE CHURCH FASCINATING, CHALLENGING, AND TRANSFORMATIVE IS THAT PARTICULARITY IS MAINTAINED *WITHIN AND BECAUSE OF* THE UNITY OF SUBMITTING TO CHRIST'S LORDSHIP.

church and proudly proclaims that he is going to start a ministry in your church that will mow lawns in the neighborhood at no charge to the residents. On its face, it sounds like a good thing. He has a particular desire and particular lawn-mowing skills, so everything sounds great. As the ministry takes shape, though, he instructs those working with him to dump the lawn clippings and yard waste they've collected in the front yard of a man in his neighborhood with whom he has recently had a dispute. Doing as they are instructed, the ministry partners dump the clippings and kill the man's lawn.

When church leaders hear of this, they speak to the lawn-mowing ministry leader and ask why he did such a thing. "Because that's what I felt I needed to do" was his reply.

We know that this is a ridiculous example, and perhaps one of the reasons it strikes us as such is the man's audacity to do something so cruel. Problematically, we see that the lawn-mowing man has no problem with particularity. The ministry was his idea and no one else's. He alone had the skill and equipment. But his desire and particularity did not come under Christ's lordship. At some level, this man got particularity right—but unity wrong. His desire to mow lawns was fine, but that desire first needed to be God-oriented if his particularity was not going to be a divisive presence in the church.

It's this kind of "both-and" that we think can be really, really good news for both those who are wondering if the church still has a place for them and for the church, which really does need those who are a bit more particular, even if the church doesn't always realize it right away. We're going to come back to this "both-and" of the church a bit later, but we have a few more steps to take.

## ARE YOU A PERSON?

It's pretty amazing that the words of Paul's writing so long ago still carry so much applicability to the situation in which we are in today. Whether we realize it or not, there is still a lively conversation being had about Paul's principles, and it's playing out in the media, politics, human rights campaigns, education, and just about every other public forum in the Western world. It's the idea of what makes a person.

Now, to give a little background, there was a time when humans would have naturally assumed that we are communal beings. In Paul's day, for example, people tended to think of themselves as being members of a community or communion first rather than being free-spirited, uncommitted individual beings. Over time, however, philosophers began trying to determine if there was anything we could ever know for sure without any amount of speculation. One philosopher, Rene Descartes, believed that there was at least one thing he could know for sure. After examining everything he thought he knew, he realized that he was relying on conjecture or speculation at some level. The lights in the sky at night, for example, were supposedly distant stars, but without firsthand experience of them, there was some amount of conjecture that was needed in knowing they were stars. Finally, he determined that the only thing he could know without any amount of speculation was that he was a thing that was thinking. That's all he knew firsthand. You might know his famous conclusion as the well-known phrase "I think—therefore I am."[1]

Descartes is a name in the history books, a philosopher who we sometimes think doesn't have a whole lot to do with us, until we realize that his legendary turn of phrase has actually shaped the way that we think about ourselves today and the way that most of our Western society functions. After Descartes, humans tended to start thinking of themselves less as members of a community and more as individual beings who were free from the connections and constraints of communities. After all, if we are primarily thinking beings, then the other people who live in my community with me really don't have much to do with who I am. I can be a thing that thinks, and I don't need anyone else to do that.

HUMANS TENDED TO START THINKING OF THEMSELVES LESS AS MEMBERS OF A COMMUNITY AND MORE AS INDIVIDUAL BEINGS WHO WERE FREE FROM THE CONNECTIONS AND CONSTRAINTS OF COMMUNITIES.

Because I'm a visual person, here's a diagram that illustrates how we live together according to this kind of outlook:

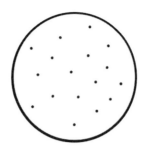

Notice that the dots don't touch one another. There are no necessary connections or relationships between them. They really don't need
one another. They are total and complete individuals. If we are honest
with ourselves, this really tends to be the way we think of ourselves
sometimes. We love our total lack of commitment and external ties to
others. I love the fact that if I don't want to do something, I don't necessarily have to do it. Or, in other words, no one else can really make a
claim on me, because I am a total and complete individual.

One of our underlying assumptions of this book, however, is that
this isn't really satisfying to most of us. Even at an unspoken level,
we want to be claimed by something larger, to be part of something
bigger, to give our lives to something other than to ourselves. Over the
last few decades, philosophers, theologians, and sociologists have been
observing a kind of shift away from Descartes' understanding of the
world and our place in it. Most philosophers have said that Descartes
launched the modern era—an era of individuality, of liberty and freedom from any kind of external constraint. But in the shift away from
Descartes and modernity, there seems to be a longing stirring in the
hearts and minds of those who are lonely, who are ready to be claimed
by something bigger than themselves and to reunite with others. As
we look around the world, we tend to see that many of those in our
generation desire something more than individuality and a life-unto-
self. It's a shift that, while cliché, is called *post-modernity*.

One of the aspects of this emerging shift is what we are going to
call the shift from understanding ourselves as individuals to understanding ourselves as persons. What in the world is the difference?

Here's a diagram that might help illustrate what this shift may look like:

Rather than being made up of completely individual and autonomous beings, persons are those who share life in a profound web of relationality. There are connections everywhere between persons. In fact, a person is a being who actually depends upon others to be who he or she is. In this model, we really do depend on others to be who we are.

If you really think about it, no one can live in total isolation. At some level or another, we depend on other persons to be who we are. From the beginning of life, we depend on our parents to conceive us, feed us, and clothe us. As we grow, we depend on others—even our own age—to teach us. Even our patterns of thought depend upon learning language, and language isn't something we can formulate on our own. We need others to be who we are. We depend on them, even for our very ability to think.

Our economic life, too, is showing us how interrelated and dependent upon one another we are. As California natives, we love fresh fruit, especially the kind that grows in the fertile San Joaquin Valley of California. Peaches are among our favorites, but there are also grapes, oranges, lemons, almonds, walnuts, apples, pomegranates, and more that grows nearby.

We love to eat everything we just listed, but we also know that we come to depend on lots of other people to be able to have them. We depend on the farmers to grow the crops, we depend on the pickers to harvest them, we depend on the truckers to haul them, and we depend on the grocer to stock them on the shelves so that we can take them home with us. The web of dependency doesn't stop there. Even the farmer depends on others to bring fertilizer, to provide farm equipment, to refine the fuel that powers the equipment, and so on. The most reclusive hermits also depend on others. We couldn't help but think that the "double rainbow" man of YouTube fame who lived in the California wilderness alone on an organic farm, the picture of solitude, depended on a host of technicians, engineers, and workers to provide him with the camera and Internet technology he used to become the "double rainbow" man of YouTube fame.

So what does any of this have to do with making room in the church for those who are wondering if there is any room left? Let's go back for a moment to the concept of homogenization. First, if we really are individuals, it means we don't need others to be who we are. It means, to use Paul's language, that we really can tell the foot that we have no need of it and that we can go on happily as an eye.

Second, it means that it becomes awfully easy for us to homogenize others, to erase their particularity and to group them into nebulous masses under a clever title or label, because as individuals, none of them have any claim upon us. We are not related to them in any fundamental or meaningful way, so it becomes very easy for us to dismiss them. Quite simply, if we are all individuals, we don't need them.

The problem we see in the American churches these days, however, is that when we operate in this way, we start believing that we don't need the particularity of others, and it becomes pretty easy for us to dismiss them or crowd them out altogether. If others have absolutely no claim to make upon us, it becomes all the more simple to withhold hospitality from them, to turn away, and to effectively be sure that they no longer have a place at the table. This can happen in a number of ways, but the point at which we are most concerned is that it's happening to a generation who doesn't happen to have a lot of power or authority in their churches these days.

It's happening to people like our friend Rick, mentioned earlier, who desperately wants to serve, is graced and gifted for ministry in the church, is a dedicated and faithful follower of Christ, but doesn't look like the typical pastor or servant and is left wondering if there is a place for him at the table. The particularity of his look, the particularity of his journey—of his calling, of his race, of his age—all looked very unhomogenized.

For now, we should remember that Paul writes "There is neither Jew nor Gentile, neither slave nor free, nor is there male and female, for you are all one in Christ Jesus" (Galatians 3:28). But that doesn't mean we do not bring those things that make us particular into the Body of Christ. Paul is telling us that we are defined by Christ, not by our gender, social status, or heritage. But it is exactly because of our diversity that Christ works such an amazing transformation—not amalgamation—of unity.

It's also happening in Reetu's story that we told earlier. As part of her story, Reetu recognized that even though she once loathed her Indian heritage, being Indian is the only way she can be truly Christian. So she brings her particularity and offers it up to be used in God's mission of redemption for the world. After graduation from college, Reetu plans on working at Shepherd Community Center, connected with the Shepherd Community Church of the Nazarene, in a very diverse area of Indianapolis. She told us that she feels called to disciple people of diverse cultures who are new to the faith.

THE CHURCH MUST REALIZE THAT WE NEED OTHERS AT THE TABLE TO BE WHO WE ARE: THE BODY OF CHRIST UNDER THE LORDSHIP OF CHRIST— EYES, FEET, AND ALL.

"I never had a mentor to talk me through everything I went through, and I want to be that someone for someone else," she said. "I never had anyone to ask, 'Should I leave behind all aspects of my culture? Can I still celebrate Indian holidays even though they celebrate Indian gods?'" For a few years, Reetu tried to hide the part of her story that was about being Indian. But now she lives by the motto "no more hiding,"—not from her faith and not from her heritage. "Growing up trying to juggle two cultures and learning to be Christian, that's what I have to offer," she said.

In what we're hoping, the church's instinct would be to see particularity as an offering, or as a gift of living together in the community of the church. It is a hope to make a space for our friend at the table rather than attempt to erase the particularity of his or her journey, because the Church realizes that we need others at the table to be who we are: the Body of Christ under the lordship of Christ—eyes, feet, and all.

## THE SHAPE OF GOD

At the beginning of this chapter we promised you some theology, and we don't want to let you down. Again, you don't have to be an accomplished theologian to continue reading, but we can't get away from it, because the Church is a theological body. Even more, we think there is some pretty extraordinary hope for the Church and for those who are wondering if they have a place in the Church in what we are about to propose.

First, the nutshell: the God who has called the Church into existence is a God who is actually a communion of unity and particularity. If the Church is going to reflect the image of the God who has called it into being, the Church ought to take seriously the image of that God. That image is Trinity.

Let's start with imagination. It's no mistake that the word "image" shares a common root with "imagination." When we imagine something, it's not that we necessarily make it up like a fantasy, but it's the way we hold images in our minds that then go on to shape the way we actually think and act. So if we were to ask you what image of God you have in mind, that image would ultimately go on to shape the way we think and act. There have been some recent studies in which researchers have asked children to draw God, and the images they produce correspond to the way those children grow up and act.[2]

If their drawings depicted a big, commanding, and frightening God, the children's lives tended to be marked by a sense of awe and reverence. If God was drawn as kind of buddy, the children's lives tended to be marked by a playful attitude toward God. We are suggesting that it's no different for adults. The images we have in mind for God, even if we aren't aware of it, make a difference in the way we live out our lives in response, especially in the church.

Now here is one of the main points we're going to make in this chapter: most of our churches today tend to operate with an image of God that looks a lot like the individual we described earlier rather than like a person. In other words, God is an individual free of external constraint, commanding, willing, and acting totally free of any other person. Usually, this image is accompanied by the white-guy-in-a-white-beard motif. And even if we know that God isn't a big white guy with a long white beard, we tend to unconsciously attribute some of those characteristics to Him, so that He's a kind of solitary figure in the heavens, dishing out commands, blessings, and curses in a bit of an arbitrary way.

Make no mistake: this has major implications for the way our churches come to operate on a day-to-day basis. If our theological imaginations hold an image of God as an individual, then our life as the church together tends to be marked by that as well. Or, in different words, if the church is called to be the image of God on earth, and God is an individual, guess what our churches tend to look like.

As we've already said, once we are a collection of individuals, it tends to be a lot easier to dismiss others, thinking that we don't need them to be who we are, in the same way that God as an individual doesn't need anything or anyone else to be who He is. The white guy with the white beard is alone in heaven.

But according to the Christian faith, that isn't the image of God Christians should have in their theological imaginations. Instead, the God of Christian faith takes on a totally different shape, an image that is completely unique to Christianity, and an image, we think, that can offer a lot of hope for those wondering if there is room for them in church anymore.

This shape is Trinity, the strange and beautiful confession that God is not an individual but actually a communion of three divine persons—persons who are particular but who live in unity as one God.

This image of God was something stoked in the theological imaginations of early Christians who were trying to make sense of what they had seen when they encountered Jesus and when they had seen His ministry, life, death, resurrection, and ascension. How could someone who was so human, who walked and ate and slept and died, also be divine? Some early theologians tried to make sense of what they had seen by suggesting that Jesus had just appeared to be human but that He was actually divine.

The problem there was that if Jesus weren't human, it didn't really matter for us humans, because if God had not truly become human, then God hadn't really assumed our problems and our brokenness and therefore couldn't really do a whole lot about healing and restoring us from destruction to wholeness. Other theologians suggested that Jesus was in "parts," that His body was human but His mind was really divine. However, again there was the problem that if Jesus weren't *wholly* human, that if His mind were not human, our minds can't be truly healed, because God had not really assumed humanity in its fullness.

THE SHAPE AND NATURE OF THE TRINITY SUGGESTS TO US THAT GOD IS NOT HOMOGENEOUS BUT THAT HE IS ACTUALLY THREE PARTICULAR DIVINE PERSONS WHO MAKE UP A UNIFIED COMMUNION.

To make matters a bit more complex, there was also this experience that Christians had of firsthand encounters with a Spirit who did more than give them warm feelings but actually began to transform their thoughts, their attitudes, and their beliefs, opening the way and guiding them toward believing what Jesus really was what God was doing to heal the world. It was going to take some very out-of-the-box descriptions of God to be able to make sense of all this. As it turned out, early Christians realized they couldn't use "either-or" language to describe what they had experienced, what had been revealed to them. Instead, they opted to use descriptions that allowed "both-and" language that maintained that Jesus was human *and* divine and that the Spirit they had experienced was distinct but not separate from the God of creation.

If you're having a bit of a difficult time wrapping your head around how this all works, don't despair—it took years for early Christians to find the right words to put a description on this theological reality that we call the Trinity—and we're still searching for words that will help us understand just a bit more fully what is actually going on with the Trinity. What we would like to highlight, though, is that the image of God as Trinity actually helps us to be the church more faithfully, to resist the urge to imagine God as a sheer individual who then calls us to be individuals too. Here's how:

First, the shape and nature of the Trinity suggests to us that God is not homogeneous but that He is actually three particular divine persons who make up a unified communion as one God. Second, that image suggests to us there's something about being made in God's image that means we ought to look a little something like this triune God, so we ought not to be homogeneous but a communion of particular persons. Finally, the shape of a triune God suggests that God's very being is that of love, and that if we are going to be the image of God on earth, our lives together ought to be lives in love as well.

The first way the Trinity suggests to us a more faithful way of being the Church is that God is not homogeneous but actually three particular persons who make up a unified communion as one God. If the notion of "person" is troubling to you, especially in trying to describe God, let us say that we can understand such confusion. We tend to use the word *person* to describe humans, and we aren't really talking about humans when it comes to the Trinity.

But this is a word that has some incredible implications for us. First, it's probably the best word we have to describe what we've experienced as those who have encountered God through Christ and the Holy Spirit. Second, we tend to think that a person is a total and complete individual, that a person is one who can live alone, who needs no one else to be who he or she is, and these ideas tend to confuse us when it comes to talking about the triune God as persons. Our hope for us is that our language will begin to take on the shape of the theological reality we've experienced so that "person" doesn't simply mean a completely autonomous individual but rather a being who lives in relation and communion with others.

Now, if the theological reality of the Trinity has anything to do with our human life, especially in the church, we would also like to suggest that we try to adjust our understanding of God to accommodate the trinitarian shape of who God is. When we use the term *God*, we usually have an image come online in our imaginations of the man with the white beard. That's all fine and good until we have to start trying to make sense of what happened with Jesus. As any kid in Sunday School will tell you, God sent Jesus. But again, there are more images of this solitary Man sending another solitary Man to earth. God is the one who does the sending, and then there's Jesus, who gets sent. The same thing tends to apply to the Holy Spirit, at least in terms of God being the big man with the white beard who remains big and white and does all the sending. In other words, when we think of God, we think of an individual. Visually, it might look something like this:

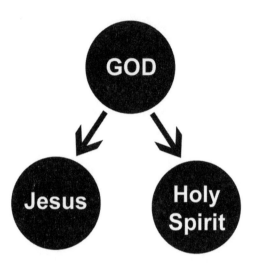

In what we're suggesting, however, "God" is the name that we give to the whole package of Father, Son, and Holy Spirit. If we take this idea of the Trinity seriously, it says to us that the only God we know is a God who is a divine communion comprised of the Father, the Son, and the Holy Spirit. In other words, God isn't an individual— God is a communion—Three in One. Visually, here's what we think it might look like.

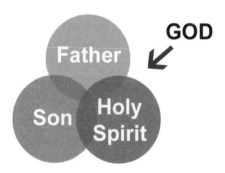

Now, this might all sound as if we're just splitting theological hairs, but we think it really could have a huge impact on the way that we're the church together and the way the church sometimes falls into the temptation to use language to homogenize, divide, and exclude. If our theological imaginations are really formed by the first diagram—if we really believe that God is an individual who simply acts and wills and sends and so on—that begins to work its way into our theological imagination in the way that we are the church together. It means that there is a likeness between God, who is an individual, and church members and leaders, who are individuals, who can will, command, and send, just as the God they imagine. There is no distinction in this model—no particularity—and communion isn't as much a way of life as much as it is a sometimes cumbersome and unnecessary side aspect of life as the church.

But if we were to take the doctrine of the Trinity seriously, if we were to allow such a strange and beautiful confession of who God is to really impact our theological imagination, we would see that God is a communion of love. Yes, there are persons who are particular and distinct, but these persons have their life as a communion, and they live in no other way. In this communion there are distinctions between the persons. Theologically speaking, the Father does the sending and the Son is sent, and this makes them distinct. The Son became flesh, the Father did not, and this makes them distinct. Yet they are absolutely unified because their life is a life-in-communion. Theologians have gone as far as to say that they are of the same "substance," meaning that even though they are distinct, they are also forever unified in a close communion. Our God is three *and* one.

If this is the image of God that begins to form our theological imagination, we hope, pray, and think that it will begin to help us be the Church together more faithfully. If we as the Church are to be made in God's image, the image of God we have in mind goes a long way in how we are the Church together; so my hope is that this strange and beautiful image of God as a communion of love will begin to shape the way we are the Church together. As we mentioned earlier, there's something about being made in God's image that means we ought to look a little something like this triune God, so we ought not be homogeneous but a communion of particular persons.

What might this look like? There's no way we can extrapolate everything that we think this theological shift suggests to us, but I do think that, at the very least, we will begin to move from thinking of ourselves as a loose collection of individuals and more as a communion of persons. In that communion, however, the persons are not homogenized; they do not all need to be exactly alike and their distinctions become a necessary part of their communion together. In other words, they must remain particular. The moment they lose their particularity, they become homogenized, and the kind of communion that we have in mind here collapses.

The NBC show *Community* takes a pretty hilarious jab at the notion of homogenization and the idea that we can and should try to erase particularity. The show is about an unlikely group of misfits who become friends at a community college. The college is undergoing a mascot change, and like so many schools in real life, they are trying to avoid any character that might offend or prefer any one group of students. This comical mascot search ends with the dean of the school introducing the newly minted Greendale Community College Human Being. Out walks a person in leotards that cover every inch of the body in an unnatural grey fabric with nearly indistinguishable facial features faintly drawn over an ambiguous shape of the human body that seems neither male nor female.

The irony, of course, is that in the attempt not to offend any one group of people, they've come up with a creature whose total and complete lack of any particular features has made it freakishly inhuman—an offense to the entire human race.

The more serious question raised from such a humorous parody, however, is whether or not we can really be a communion in the absence of particularity. If we take a cue from the doctrine of the Trinity, it seems that particularity isn't something to be clothed by nebulous leotards in a freakish attempt to make us all the same, but to allow the particularity of our experience to shape the community of the Church. Such a community is one primarily obedient and submitted to Christ in such a way that God's healing and redemptive power is present and evident, and also in such a way that space is opened to those who are seeking a seat at the table.

For those of us who are wondering if there is a place in the church for us, questioning whether or not there's a place at the table, we would say first that a church in the image of the triune God must make a place for you. The communion of the church is not the communion if it is dismissing particularity for the sake of homogeneity. Many organizational growth experts will tell you that the fastest-growing institutions are those that are homogeneous, because in those institutions growth isn't hindered by the problems of difference and dissention. The problem we have with that kind of approach is that it doesn't seem to model a God who is triune—it seems to want to model a God who is homogeneous, and that isn't the God who has been revealed to us. It's our hope that the church will stand ready to model a God who is particularity-in-communion, to make a space for those who seek to worship Christ in their particular and peculiar ways.

That doesn't mean that our particular desires and ideas will always remain exactly as they are, and we think that this is actually good news. In fact, it's redemptive news. When our particularity is submitted to the lordship of Christ, it's transformed and redeemed, but not erased. Those desires that need to be reoriented toward God are, those thoughts that need to be directed toward divine ends are, and through God's powerful grace, all our particularity is transformed into God's original and perfect purpose. Our particularity is not washed away, but the good desires we have are simply reoriented toward God's conclusion, and our desires, impulses, and passions come to serve redemptive and healing purposes. If you've been around the church very long, you might have heard this referred to as *sanctification*.

We think this could be some really good news for those who are seeking a place in the church but are struggling to find one, or wondering if there is even a place left in the church at all. As we've said before, one of the real challenges we face is a temptation to homogenize entire segments, to lump them all together and dismiss them as if we didn't need them at all. In the conversations we've had with those who struggle to find a place in the church, and in our own struggles to find a place, there is often the common theme of being homogenized by another group as "young people" and then being dismissed because "young people" are troublesome with their desire to change things, their radical politics, and so on. But we think the church does those things when its theological imagination gets stale, or, in other words, it fails to see the incredible possibilities presented to us when we take seriously the idea that the God who has called the church into being is a God who is a communion of love. That God is a God of distinct persons who cannot homogenize, label, and dismiss one another.

# A SAD DAY
# 8       AT
# SAFEWAY

**THE CHRISTMAS** decorations were still up around the house when
we first heard the news that there had been a shooting in Arizona.
"What's going on in Arizona?" Shawna's sister asked, her phone in
hand, checking her Facebook news feed. "Everyone's posting about it."

When we turned on the television set and found a news channel,
the commentators were already talking about a potential motive for
the shooting. "Could this have been politically motivated?" one com-
mentator asked a guest, who responded that it's certainly a possibility. The next day, Pima County Sheriff Clarence Dupnik gave a press
conference in which he made the provocative claim that the shooting
somehow had to do with the way we were talking to one another.

"I think with the vitriolic rhetoric we hear day in and day out
from people in the radio business and some people in the television
business and what [we] see on television and how our youngsters are
being raised, that this has not become the nice United States that most
of us grew up in," he said. The final words of his statement were probably what grabbed my attention more than anything else: "I think it's
time that we do some soul-searching."

We couldn't really help but wonder how someone would take it upon themselves to pick up a gun and commit such an act of violence against so many innocent people. But at the same time, we also couldn't help but think a bit on what this might mean for the Church and how the Church doesn't seem to be all that immune from the same kinds of divisions that Sheriff Dupnik had identified. Granted, there were many who disagreed with Dupnik in attributing the shooting in Tucson to "vitriolic rhetoric," but the point wasn't entirely lost as the national conversation began to turn toward the kind of rhetoric that we had been using in describing one another, particularly those who were different from us in some way, be it politically, ideologically, or even theologically. Again, we couldn't help but think of the Church.

OUR LANGUAGE WAS SHAPING THE REALITY OF THE LONG-TIMERS FROM THE NEW FOLKS, THE CONSERVATIVES FROM THE LIBERALS, THE NEIGHBORHOOD KIDS FROM THE SUBURB KIDS.

We couldn't help being reminded of the hard conversations we had recently had with others in the church, or the way they had spoken to us, or the language they had used to describe others. As we saw in Kassidy's story, all of it seemed as if it began to shape our imaginations in such a way that the divides between people became more polarized, and suddenly our word choice was actually putting up real barriers between members of our church. Our language was shaping the reality of the long-timers from the new folks, the conservatives from the liberals, the neighborhood kids from the suburb kids—there were quite a few "us" and "them" kinds of statements that actually started to shape the way we associated at church.

There's a phrase that Tim likes to use when he's talking about ethics with the college students he teaches. He uses it intentionally, because he think it helps them make sense of ethics as being more than a list of what is permissible or not based on some abstract philosophical principle. He talks a lot to them about *moral imagination*.

He loves the phrase because it defies the kind of ethics that college students are often drawn toward—the kind that is nothing more than a clean calculation where you input a problem, run it through a kind of moral calculator, and come out on the other side with a neat and perfectly reasonable solution to the issue. The problem we have with doing ethics that way is that it doesn't seem to really apply to the world we see around us. We don't tend to see many neatly cut solutions to the problems we face that tie up all the loose ends in a tidy package.

So Tim talks a lot to his students about doing ethics a bit differently. He talks about doing the kind of ethics that get back to the original meaning of the word *ethos*, which is a Greek word we usually translate as *character*. In other words, he's much more interested in developing a deep sense of character in his students than with them becoming efficient moral calculators. Because there are so rarely neat and tidy answers to situations we encounter on a day-to-day basis, he's more interested in equipping them with a vivid moral imagination, the kind that can envision possibilities that others couldn't imagine—an imagination that can see the world in terms of brilliant, colorful possibilities rather than simplistic, black-and-white, calculated solutions.

So what's the connection here? What does moral imagination have to do with the way we talk to each other in the church? It's because the language we use in speaking to and about each other begins to shape our moral and theological imaginations. In fact, it begins to shape the kind of character formed within us, leading us to be able to view possibilities that we may not have been able to see before.

If we could use a bit of what might seem like a radical example for a minute, I hope it will clarify where we're going with this idea. In most of the American history classes I took in middle school and high school, the civil rights era of the 1960s seems like it was thousands of years ago. In most lessons our teachers presented to our classes, there was a kind of underlying message: *Aren't we glad that we would never do such a thing today? Aren't we glad that this is in the past and that we don't treat one another like this anymore? I'm sure we could never be like those who supported racial segregation and oppression. We've developed way beyond that.*

There are certainly times we wonder how life could have come to that in so recent a past. On this side of history, we are often dismayed at how many people thought those kinds of actions and policies were permissible and good. But there are also times we wonder if people who were living in the midst of those times had any sense that something was wrong with what they were doing. We can look at them from this side of history and quietly congratulate ourselves for not being as harmful as they were, but we do wonder what makes us so different from them.

To begin, let us say that we're not entirely sure there is much that's different between us and those who fought to keep society racially segregated or those who rallied lynch mobs. They probably had many of the same concerns we have today: to see this world become a better place, to be able to grow up and have a "happily ever after," to find meaning and value in life.

So how did it all go so wrong? What made them believe so deeply that the world is better as long as African-Americans were forced to eat in different restaurants than Caucasians and ride in the backs of public buses? There were many factors, obviously, but the one we would like to point toward now is the kind of language that was used, especially the kind of language that was used by Caucasians who wanted to maintain a racially segregated society. The language they used, the ways they spoke to and about one another, began forming within them a character—an *ethos*—that gave silent permission for segregationist policies and actions. In fact, if you think of any conflict between groups of people, one of the most common factors is that one group will often use derogatory names to describe the other. Over time, that language begins to form within us and those around us a character that is all too ready to live into the reality that this kind of language creates. Often the reality of our social lives begins to take on the reality that our language had ascribed to it long before. Language shapes character, and character becomes the basis for what we understand to be allowable in terms of our actions toward each another.

Philosophers sometimes talk about this as what they call a "hermeneutical circle," in which we attempt to use language to describe something, but that description shapes the reality we are describing just a bit, which in turn leads to another description, which further shapes the reality. If these philosophers are right, and we tend to think

> LANGUAGE SHAPES CHARACTER, AND CHARACTER BECOMES THE BASIS FOR WHAT WE UNDERSTAND TO BE ALLOWABLE IN TERMS OF OUR ACTIONS TOWARD EACH ANOTHER.

they are, language is far more than a tool for description. It actually has a very, very powerful function in shaping the way we think and the way we imagine. The language we use shapes our character, so that when we are faced with certain situations, the language that has been shaping us begins to dictate the possibilities open to us in that situation. Though there was a lot going on in the life of the Tucson shooter, maybe Sheriff Supnik touched on something true. Maybe the kind of combative language that had been used in the political arena suggested to a troubled young man that several political figures really were his enemy. The language he heard time and time again may have done something to shape his character, to open the door to a violent possibility, as unthinkable as that possibility may have seemed to so many others.

So where is all of this heading? Obviously, we're talking about the Church. The Church, while being a gift from God, is still a gathering of humans, as we know all too well. Gatherings of humans have a way of relating to one another through language, language that often starts being used in the hopes of describing a reality that already exists but often carries an interpretation of that reality and begins to actually shape that reality in the end. In other words, the language we use in human association, even the Church, has the character of opening possibilities that may have seemed unimaginable to us previously.

In October 2006 Charles Carl Roberts, who was thirty-two years old at the time, went to a schoolhouse in rural Lancaster County, Pennsylvania, and opened fire on ten innocent girls who belonged to the nearby Amish community before turning the gun on himself. At the time, it seemed to us to be yet another senseless tragedy, another deranged killer, another group of mourning families. But as the story began unfolding, we were shocked by the way the community handled the situation. When the news media arrived on the scene that evening, they learned that less than seven hours after the shooting, a representative of the Amish community came to the house of the shooter to offer the community's forgiveness to him and his family. Rather than making demands, threats, or insults, the community was strangely capable of imagining another possibility, of seeing another option on the table, and acted in a way that was completely different than any possibility that we were capable of imagining when we heard about the situation. A deep character had been formed in the community that came to light in the language they used to describe the situation and the man who committed the act. "In my heart I've forgiven him," said the grandfather of two girls killed in the attack.[1]

In all the material we were able to find on the incident, we couldn't find an interview with a member of the community who referred to Roberts as a killer or anything worse. Instead, the language used to describe him was laced with the language of forgiveness. What we began to realize was that the language used to describe the situation formed a character that opened the possibility for a response other than retaliation or bitter anger. Surprisingly, there was now another option on the table: that of mourning and forgiveness.

While we were growing up in the church, there were probably many times we heard language being used of others, whether it be a group in the church or outside the church, that was less than helpful. If you've grown up in the church, this probably won't come as a surprise, but there were times when the language being used was just downright *divisive*.

As a young teenager, Tim longed for something he could relate to at church. The services were fine but rarely captured his imagination. He saw that other churches nearby had turned a kind of aesthetic corner and were using music, art, liturgy, and creative expression in ways that seemed light years from where we were as a congregation. When he saw what they were doing, something within him responded at a guttural level—he profoundly wanted to express his love and adoration for God in ways that invoked creativity and imagination. And when some of us expressed our desire for movement toward this kind of worship, there was quite a bit of resistance, mainly from the older generation, who desperately wanted to keep things as they were because that's how they learned to worship, and they genuinely resonated with everything we saw as stale.

"We could actually do something interesting once in a while," another teenager said to Tim one day after church, "if the blue-hairs would actually do something other than collect dust on a pew and tell us we can't do anything creative." It wasn't a particularly innovative affront, but the name stuck, at least with those of us who were young. In fact, we had never considered the blue-hairs to be much of a problem until they had a name. Now the entire group had a title, and under that title Tim was able to quickly gather them up and dismiss them as irrelevant, out of touch, and difficult to deal with. In fact, once they had a name, Tim found all kinds of possibilities that hadn't been open to him before. He didn't know he could resent those who had given so much of their own lives to pass on a legacy of faith until they became the blue-hairs. He didn't know that he could so easily dismiss the particularity of their experiences and personalities until they became the blue-hairs. In fact, he didn't realize how obstinate and uncompromising a group of people could be until they were all gathered together under one title.

UNTIL THEY WERE THE BLUE-HAIRS, WE WERE A CONGREGATION TOGETHER. NOW THERE WERE FACTIONS.

The title made it incredibly simple for Tim. The church was broken, and it was *their* fault. The church was unimaginative, and *they* were making it that way. Though he had spent his entire life in the church, it wasn't until then that he saw the blue-hairs as being *other* from himself. Until they were the blue-hairs, we were a congregation together. Now there were factions. The longer Tim's group began to use the language they had invented to describe another group in the church, a couple things began happening simultaneously: first, it served to form them into a group—to unite us around a common language, and second, it began to shape the reality of our life with the blue-hairs. The very act of grouping a collection of people under language of our invention by its very nature began forming within us a character of division, complete with a set of possibilities that were quite unhelpful and less than charitable. This kind of character formation was the result of the language we used, and for the first time we were presented with the possibilities of dismissing, marginalizing, and forsaking a significant percentage of our congregation.

We're not entirely sure the church always has the eyes to see this today. Sometimes we find ourselves wondering if we are doing ourselves a service in the church, or if we are creating problems for ourselves, when we gather the church into sub-groups under creative titles. We do see value in things like age-level ministry, but there are times, when we begin to name other groups in the church, that we fear we have opened the door to a set of possibilities that had never occurred to us before, things like dismissal, marginalization, and even more divisive kinds of attitudes, born out of the language that has shaped the reality of our life together as members of Christ's Body.

Another reality that language can shape, especially in the church, is what we've already identified as homogenization. As the process of taking things that may be different and making them all alike, homogenization washes away all distinctive aspects and erases particularity of persons. Once we have titles, once we can gather entire groups of people into neat categories, it becomes a temptation of our modern and scientific minds to attempt to ascribe grand patterns to these groups.

Recently we were invited to a church leadership meeting in which the leaders of the church gathered to talk about how the different ministries of the church could and should function together. As was the case for our particular church, the leadership began to look around the room and realized there were very few young people, that actually there were only three who were under forty-five in the room. The conversation that unfolded was fascinating.

"We've got to have more service opportunities," one leader said boldly, "because young people like service opportunities."

Another leader suggested a different approach: "We need to have more for children, because that will bring in younger people."

In all of the pitches for what we heard, it was entirely possible that the category of "young people" was a kind of homogeneous gathering of people who are all alike in some way, who all have similar desires and will all be inspired to give their lives to something greater because the church leadership applies a single, magic approach. What seemed to be missing from the conversation was any kind of attention to the particularity of persons.

Now, just so we are being clear, this phenomenon isn't only something we've seen in the church of the older generation to the younger generation. Instead, what we're talking about is the tendency we have to apply categories through the application of our language and then create realities in which we have little choice but to homogenize the entire group we have created through our language. In fact, what Tim had done as a teenager was entirely similar. He had chosen language that created a reality of homogenized blue-hairs, all alike, all problematic, all unnecessary. The problem here is that his language didn't necessarily allow him to see beyond the homogenization that had taken place and into particular gifts that certain persons were to him or to the rest of the congregation, precisely because they had been homogenized into a group that Tim had already dismissed.

Now if sociologists are right, and we tend to think they are, there are certainly distinctive markers between generations in things like preferences, attitudes, and outlooks on particular issues. We aren't going to try to suggest that there aren't general differences between generations, but we are going to suggest that the church is unique on theological grounds and that as a distinctive and rare body, such distinctions shouldn't define our fellowship. We would much rather suggest that we begin to examine the language we use to describe one another in the church and let certain theological realities begin to shape our language, which will then in turn shape the realities of our communion together, such that space is made for those who previously had felt as if there was no longer a place for them in the church.

WHAT ABOUT THE LANGUAGE WE USE OF ONE ANOTHER? COULD IT BE THAT THE CHARACTER FORMED BY OUR LANGUAGE COULD TAKE ON THE IMAGE OF GOD?

If we're going to be able to get at what we've just described above, if the church can adjust its language to match its theological confessions so that we can resist homogenization and dismissal of entire age groups, we would like to suggest that our theological imaginations need a Trinitarian adjustment. In the previous chapter we suggested that the image of God that we hold in mind makes a difference for the way we live together as the church. The way we imagine God shapes the way we imagine the church and in turn the way the church is shaped. But what about the language we use of one another? Could it be that the character formed by our language could take on the image of God?

One of the hopeful aspects we see in recovering the strange and beautiful vision of God that is Trinitarian is that our language can indeed take on the image of God. Rather than being a tool to homogenize and dismiss others, a Trinitarian theological imagination could actually recover the idea that we are beings in communion with one another, particular and unified in that communion. Once our imaginations are stoked to view the church as a communion in the image of a triune God, our language can begin to take on that reality. Suddenly, our language will take on the shape of a communion of persons who realize they need one another and deeply value one another's particularity.

Our hope is that this kind of shift in language will actually be able to open spaces of hospitality and welcome, that the words we use to describe each another will actually become the means by which those who are wondering if they have a place in the church will be invited to the party. It's our hope that when we take particularity and unity seriously we will be less inclined to describe entire groups in wide terms, because we see particular persons rather than frustrating liabilities. It's our hope that this kind of shift could reach out to a teenager like the one Tim was and present to him a possibility that he hadn't been able to imagine before: that the blue-hairs were not a group that could be gathered together and written off, but that he needed them deeply, that their stories, experiences, desires, and worship were something that was a gift to the communion.

As for a generation who now wonders if it has a seat at the table, we are hopeful this kind of shift in theological imagination will allow the entire church to recognize the gift young people can be, not to be homogenized into what young people once looked like—but in their particularity *now*.

If we're honest, though, the problem is often a two-way street. It's not only that the older generations homogenize and dismiss the younger generations. There are often times when the younger generations homogenize and dismiss the older generations, the way Tim did as a teenager. A church in the image of a triune God is a church that cannot homogenize entire groups in the language it uses, nor can it dismiss those groups as being unnecessary or irrelevant. A church in the image of a triune God is a communion of love, a communion that necessarily upholds the particularity of persons as necessary to its life together and embodies that in its language. A church in the image of the triune God cannot say that an entire segment of its population is unnecessary, because in doing so it has done fundamental damage to its own communion. And the good news for those who are wondering if the church has any room for them anymore is this: the church needs your particularity. The church, as a communion in the image of God, cannot simply dismiss you; for when it does, it does so at the cost of its own communion.

The language we use of one another must be hospitable language if we're going to maintain a communion in the image of God. Our conversations must be holy conversations, as we spoke of earlier. Our language must resist the temptation of ascribing titles to entire segments of our communion and thus homogenizing away their particularity.

If we're to be a communion in God's image, we need the particularity of the younger generations, the older generations, the traditionalists, the progressives, the conservatives, the liberals, the accountants, the artists, the geeks, the hipsters, the grandmothers, and the newborns. If our church is to image a triune God, we must cultivate the character of communion in our language and allow our theological imaginations to be inspired by the revelation that God is not homogeneous but communal—relational and particular. And if our theological imaginations can be so inspired, it's our hope that our language will begin to create realities in our churches that reflect and image a triune God. These are realities that prompt us to find each generation precious and necessary to maintain the communion.

On a practical level, is this easy? No, it isn't. In fact, it probably means there will need to be a fundamental shift in the way we think about being the church together. It probably means that we are going to need to give up some of our opinions to make room for the particu-

IF WE'RE TO BE A COMMUNION IN GOD'S IMAGE, WE NEED THE PARTICULARITY OF THE YOUNGER GENERATIONS, THE OLDER GENERATIONS, THE TRADITIONALISTS, THE PROGRESSIVES, THE CONSERVATIVES, THE LIBERALS, THE ACCOUNTANTS, THE ARTISTS, THE GEEKS, THE HIPSTERS, THE GRANDMOTHERS, AND THE NEWBORNS.

larity of others. It probably means that we will need to see the particularity of others as a gift rather than a liability. It probably means that our own desires need to be seen as expendable when they are placed alongside an image of communion.

One of our favorite images of the Trinity found in Scripture is Jesus praying in the garden before His arrest, recorded in Luke 22. "Father, if you are willing," He prays, "take this cup from me; yet not my will, but yours be done" (Luke 22:42). In an astounding glimpse of the triune relationship, we see that this communion sometimes requires a laying down of one's own desires, even at a deep level. But this doesn't apply only to those who have little power in the church. Indeed, it applies to anyone who seeks to join into that holy and sacred communion that is the church. It means that there is a mutual laying down for one another, a giving-up of our own place and desires that Jesus models time and time again in His ministry.

John 13 gives us a look at the kind of sacrifice-in-communion we have in mind here. It's the kind where Jesus, having been given power and authority, takes on the role of a servant and washes the feet of those with whom He is in communion, even those who were actively seeking His destruction. This kind of communion isn't simply those with power maintaining things they want, but it is also those with power laying it aside for the sake of loving and serving others, much as Jesus made a place for the Canaanite woman at the table.

Again, the practical aspects of these are far from easy, but they are worth pursuing. One of the most challenging aspects of giving our language a Trinitarian shape is the way we deliberate with one another. When we had just arrived at one of the churches we served, the congregation had recently finished remodeling one of its buildings, which was now a beautiful place of worship. One of our dear friends, who had served on the committee for the remodel, pointed out one feature of the building that she had wanted included in the construction process and said, "Yeah, I won that battle." Her words stuck with us. We couldn't help but imagine what that battle must have been like, and then we couldn't help but wonder why she used that kind of language to describe the process of making aesthetic decisions about the church's worship space.

Sadly, we think her comment was probably pretty accurate in describing what deliberation often looks like in the church. It's the collision of individuals who do not need one another on a deep level. It's the battle between unrelated factions. And all of this, we fear, has something to do with the kind of theological imagination that has been developed in our churches for so long.

Deliberation doesn't need to be a battle. In fact, if our language in the church takes on the character of a theological imagination informed by a Trinitarian vision of God, we might actually find that deliberation doesn't have to be associated nearly as much with conflict. Rather than battle or conflict, deliberation takes seriously the particularity of the other person, all the while realizing that we need that person, that he or she is necessary to our communion. If we can't dismiss others, if they are necessary to our communion, how might that begin to shape our language? Our hope is that with this shift in theological imagination, the practical considerations of disagreement and deliberation don't need to take on a connotation of conflict but can instead be framed by a common unity in Christ.

When Tim is teaching college students about their discourse in class, he often talks about the difference between debate and deliberation. Debate, he tells them, is the set of tactics people employ to win their case. It doesn't necessarily have anything good or true at its core—it's simply designed to win. Tim's college roommate was a gifted debater on our school's national champion debate team. Tim would often go to watch debate matches and marvel at his roommate's ability to construct an argument and dismantle his opposition, especially when he knew that his roommate hated his own argument on a personal level. Tim's roommate probably could have won a debate even if he had to argue that it was better to kick puppies than to pet them.

Deliberation, on the other hand, has been described as two friends sitting in front of a warm fire, enjoying each other's company and holding each other accountable to the truth. It doesn't matter which friend wins as long as goodness and truth win in the end, and each partner in deliberation engages with that intent. "Let goodness carry the day," they might say at the outset of their discussion, "and as long as that happens, I'm all right with making some concessions in this conversation."

We think that we Christians have all the more reason to adjust our language away from debate and more toward deliberation, because even in the midst of disagreement, we are ultimately a communion of particular persons who are submitted to Christ and who need one another to be who we are.

## PRESENT AS PROPHETS

We've been around the church long enough to know that this isn't always (or ever) easy to accomplish. To form a communion that models the Trinity isn't always as simple as explaining it to the rest of the congregation. Often it requires what we call a prophetic presence. The biblical prophets, contrary to popular understanding, weren't fortune tellers or psychics with the ability to tell the future. Instead, they were those who were present among their people, calling them back to faithfulness. They stood in the midst of those they knew and reminded them who they were. If we're honest, sometimes the prophets were ignored, but they remained, calling, reminding, and retelling their people who they were and how God had called them to be something other.

Also, prophets tended to be a bit particular. They tended to stand out a bit, to be anything other than homogeneous. Our churches need particular prophets in their midst. Often the very presence of particular others is what's needed to remind the church that it is imaging something less than God if it is in the business of dismissing particularity. And in these situations, faithful prophets are sometimes required to step forward and, by their very presence, remind the church that it worships a God who is a God-in-communion and that it is called to be a church-in-communion.

Prophets had to be faithful, they had to be patient, they had to be submitted to God, and they had to be *present*. Have you ever started into a story that you thought would be hilarious in a group and then realize halfway through that there's someone in the group who might be offended by the story? In a way, that person is offering the storyteller a prophetic presence. They are, by their very presence, saying that a story that might be funny in a homogeneous group is probably going to use language divisively and that some adjustment is required.

The same is true of young people in the church. As a communion, the church needs the presence of young people in a prophetic capacity, to be fully present in their particularity, reminding the church that it is that unique body in the image of a triune God. The presence of prophets doesn't allow homogeneity but calls and encourages the church to look a little more like the image of a God who is a communion of particular persons united in love.

Is there a place for you at the table? Yes. There must be if the church is to be an image of the God it worships. And sometimes those who are wondering if there is still a place at the table are those who must be prophetically present to remind the rest of the church that they cannot be faithful if they are dismissing particularity.

# SET ANOTHER PLACE

9      AT THE
TABLE

TRY a Google search for *hospitality*. You'll find that not only are your search results directing you to Web sites for hotels and restaurants, but for the rest of the day the ad space in many of the Web sites you visit will try to tell you where you can go to buy the nicest meal or rent the nicest hotel room. It's a reality that makes the term "hospitality industry" rather ironic.

*Hospitality* in its essence refers to a relationship established between guest and host. At its core, the industry refers to the production and distribution of goods and services in exchange for compensation. Now imagine a host who invites you over for a time of hospitality and, at the end of your time together, hands you a bill for the tea and cake you've just shared. Hospitality isn't something you can buy, and it isn't something you can charge for. Hospitality is a gift given and received, an exchange in which room is made for someone else.

That's why we see so much potential in talking about the practices of hospitality when it comes to offering hope to those who are seeking a place in the church. Making room at the table is far more than something that is the polite thing to do—it's actually a practice that has a long history and tradition within the Christian faith. Of course, that long tradition has been co-opted by Priceline, Hilton, and Best Western. In our world, good hospitality is no longer a gift—it's for sale.

Perhaps this is why North American Christians have lost this peculiar and prophetic practice. Perhaps this is why we sometimes have a difficult time making space for the outsider in our churches. Gladly, though, we see this practice littered throughout Scripture. You may not be accustomed to making Leviticus a frequent stop in your morning devotions, but this is where we see some of the first exhortations to God's people to welcome the stranger with practices of hospitality (Leviticus 25:35). The historical books of the Bible recount how both Rahab and the widow were commended for their faith shown through providing hospitality (Joshua 2—6). David demonstrated absurd hospitality when he invited the last living relative of his enemy and predecessor, who happened to be a crippled boy, to come and sit at his table and dwell in his courts (2 Samuel 8—9). The prophet Elijah asked for hospitality when he passed through a foreign land (1 Kings 17-18). Jesus proclaimed the kingdom of God where those who were once considered outsiders are now invited in. The Pharisees were uncomfortable with Jesus' brand of hospitality. They cried, "This man welcomes sinners and eats with them" (Luke 15:2).

LEVITICUS IS WHERE WE SEE SOME OF THE FIRST EXHORTATIONS TO GOD'S PEOPLE TO WELCOME THE STRANGER WITH PRACTICES OF HOSPITALITY.

Of course, the most lavish and bizarre act of hospitality is that while we were strangers to God, obscured in our sin, Christ welcomed us into God's life with His very own. How rich an invitation that He would sit around a table, take bread, break it, and and say, "This is my body given for you" (Luke 22:19). When Christ welcomes us, He is not only the host—He is also the meal.

## BOLDLY ASKING FOR GOOD GIFTS

The story of the Canaanite woman in Matthew 15, which has been the operative text for this book, portrays a strange kind of hospitality. She comes recognizing her need and demands an invitation into Jesus' presence.

Having spent several years working with teenagers, we know what it's like to have someone enter your home without invitation or announcement, demanding your attention. One student made a frequent habit of this. And since he was a teenage boy, he was, of course, always hungry. Thinking about the Canaanite woman makes me picture this student walking into our house while we are eating dinner and saying, "Don't get up. I just want to hang out with you guys so much that I'll just sit here on the floor under the table, hoping you drop a few spaghetti noodles." And we wonder, what would we do if he had done that? Of course, we wouldn't let him just sit there on the floor. Even if he sat in total silence, his very presence would be a blaring proclamation that we had failed to welcome him.

Shawna is a part of a women's Bible study, the members of which have become very significant conversation partners in her life. Each week they sit in a living room drinking tea, reading the Bible, praying, sharing life, and drinking more tea. Most of the women are married with young children. Shawna is the baby of the group and loves her relationship with these women. When she told them about this book we were working on dealing with the theme of hospitality, Marissa spoke up.

Marissa is a Filipino woman who is five feet tall and has a six-foot-wide smile and three children—God bless her! Her bright personality exudes compassion, friendship, and care for strangers. So we were surprised when she said, "Oh, I have a confession to make about hospitality," with an exasperated tone and a roll of the eyes.

Marissa went on to explain that her husband, Brian, an anthropology professor at a nearby Christian university, received a letter from the student club for missionary kids (MKs for short). Apparently this group of MKs meets weekly to discuss cross-cultural experiences, finding home in a new culture, and just to support each other and build friendships. The group discovered that Brian and Marissa had lived in the Philippines for a few years when they were first married, and the letter explained this connection that Brian and Marissa might have with the group.

But it didn't stop there. The letter went on to request that Brian and Marissa have the whole group over to their home for dinner! Silence followed by a few tiny gasps filled the room. The women of the group had an intimate knowledge of just how much these students were asking: clearing a night on the calendar, cleaning the house, shopping for groceries beyond what it takes to feed a family of five, finding someone to watch the kids, cooking the meal, having the dinner, doing the dishes, putting the house back together. They were asking for dozens of hours of her life. And that's not to mention the risk you run as a professor who lives one mile from campus—letting a dozen homesick, displaced missionary kids know where you live.

> IT IS AUDACIOUS FOR FALLEN HUMANITY TO EXPECT GOD—WHO IS RADICALLY OTHER FROM OUR FINITE BROKENNESS—TO INVITE US TO BE HEIRS IN THE HEAVENLY KINGDOM.

"I don't want to do it!" Marissa confessed in a moment of blatant honesty. "It would be one thing if I knew these people and Brian and I did the inviting, but for them to invite themselves into our home—for dinner!" We all felt sympathetic but were quietly grateful we were not the ones with the convenient connection to the Missionary Kids club.

Marissa continued, "So I've been struggling with these feelings all week, just irked by their request. But when Shawna started talking about the Gentile woman who asked Jesus to heal her daughter in front of all his Jewish disciples, I realized her request was way more out there and socially unacceptable than these college students inviting themselves over for dinner. She was totally out of line to ask Jesus that question and to keep at Him like that. But she knew who to go to—she knew to go to Jesus."

It is audacious for fallen humanity to expect God—who is radically other from our finite brokenness—to invite us to be heirs in the heavenly Kingdom. In fact, it's absurd. What could we possibly do that would warrant such a lavish invitation? Yet for those of us who have grown up in the church, even if we didn't have many gold stars on the Sunday School attendance chart, we know where to go. We know that in Christ we have been granted access that is so far beyond anything we could achieve or earn or become worthy of.

A welcome like this is more than a little embarrassing. Think about it. In all of our sinful humiliation, Christ brings us before the Alpha and Omega, dresses us in His garments of righteousness, and gives us seats of honor. How awkward must we—warmongers, prostitutes, liars, thieves, slanderers—look in our new digs? How utterly embarrassing! Until we hear those words, those beautiful, shocking, impossible words: *Child, you are forgiven.* How quickly we forgot from whence we came! How short our memory! How finite our imagination!

As Christians, when we gather and feast on Christ's body and blood, we are invited to remember and reimagine who we are and whose we are. It is in light of this memory and imagination that we are bold to ask for good gifts. We respond to these lavishly embarrassing gifts of God by opening our lives in hospitality toward those whom God has put into our lives, especially the strangers.

## PROPHETICALLY WELCOME

The absurdity of the woman's request in Matthew 15 is a bit jarring. The image of the woman crawling around like a dog licking crumbs off the floor, while hard to envision because of how shocking it is, becomes a prophetic picture of the disparity between this Gentile woman and a Jewish man like Jesus. True hospitality can make us uncomfortable, because it is the practice of inviting a stranger to become a guest, and if we're honest, strangers make us uncomfortable. But that's exactly what's so prophetic about hospitality.

The Christian prophetic tradition is not necessarily about predictions of the future but usually has more to do with calling God's people to remember what He has called them to be and to remain faithful to that calling. Quite often, a prophetic word or picture is one that tells us the way things really are and the way they ought to be. The predictions biblical prophets make are usually a pretty obvious result of what happens when you fail to be what you are supposed to be. We talk about Martin Luther King Jr. as a prophet for our time, not because he predicted when the world would end but because he called attention to the reality of racism that so many were trying to ignore and painted a vision of the way racial relations ought to be. In essence he told us, "This is not the kind of people you are supposed to be." His August 28, 1963, "I Have a Dream" speech is prophetic precisely because when the crowd in Washington, D.C., imagined his word picture, they were acutely aware that the world they lived in was so far from King's dream—yet simultaneously inspired to make this image the new reality.

Prophetic hospitality is an image of the way Christians ought to live, painted in the midst of the people of God who are struggling to live into that reality. Even if you feel unwelcomed, hospitable practices can be downright prophetic. In the face of unwelcome, of not being offered a place at the table, practices of hospitality can expose the ways in which a community has forgotten who they are and what kind of community they are called to be. Like the Gentile woman, sometimes it takes a bold request to bring to light the fact that a person is an outsider and an absurd amount of patience to demonstrate the fact that a welcome had not been extended.

PROPHETIC HOSPITALITY IS AN IMAGE OF THE WAY CHRISTIANS OUGHT TO LIVE, PAINTED IN THE MIDST OF THE PEOPLE OF GOD WHO ARE STRUGGLING TO LIVE INTO THAT REALITY.

At the same time, we must learn from Jesus here, that when an outsider comes with "great faith" seeking healing, we ought not be content to let him or her eat the crumbs from our table. The outsider's willingness to eat the crumbs ought to be jarring to us. It ought to open our eyes to those who are in our churches or who long for a place within them. The willingness to make a bold claim and be patient while waiting for a response is prophetic, but as the church, we must also humbly remember that the prophet has a legitimate role to play when the people do not listen. In other words, the prophet can proclaim a possibility for the future in light of a community's unfaithfulness. In the case of this exploration, we wonder if the prophetic warning is that when the church does not exhibit the signs of hospitality to the stranger and outsider, the young will take their leave of the church.

It's not that the church, as a place of hospitality, welcomes any and all practices into its communion. As we've referenced earlier, a moralistic therapeutic deism that refuses to acknowledge that our desires are often badly distorted away from divine purposes is a faith that cannot offer redemption, for in this system of belief there is nothing from which we should be redeemed. If a man in the church uses a ministry to dump yard waste in the front yard of his neighbor, we rightly question his actions, as we saw in the ridiculous example from chapter 7. The church, then, is not an all-permissive communion but a communion of God's hospitality—and as such, the church ought not stand in the way or create barriers to those who seek to be near Jesus, to receive God's grace, and to live a life changed forever by Christ's healing and redemption.

To those who are wondering if there is a place for them at the church's table because they have not received a welcome, we continue to say *yes*. We know there are times in which your own presence must be prophetic. There are times in which you must make bold claims and in doing so remind the community that a welcome has been withheld. A willingness to continue to engage the church in light of a withheld welcome, we hope, will be that image that will be a prophetic reminder to the church that it is a gathering of God's people and that as a sign and symbol of God's kingdom, it is called to make space for the stranger and the alien, that they, too, could know the full joy of Christ's redemption and healing.

To those who wonder if their church is the kind of community that offers such hospitality, we challenge you and your community to prayerfully consider if there are those who have not been extended a welcome, who are being sustained on leftovers, who do not have a seat at the table—and then to join the long tradition of God's people who have offered hospitality. It is toward the application and practice of hospitality that we now turn.

## GIVING HOSPITALITY A HOME

When we think of hospitality, we often think of an act taking place in a home, and rightfully so. Hospitality is welcoming the stranger into our most intimate space, which is often, but not always, our home. In her book *Making Room: Recovering Hospitality as a Christian Tradition*, theologian Christine Pohl frames the practice of Christian hospitality as reclaiming the home as a site of ministry in partnership with the local church. To welcome others as God has welcomed us, we are called to extend an invitation not just to coffee hour in the church foyer but also into our very space for living.[1] But for many Christians in their twenties, "home" is a complicated term. Is "home" your parents' house, a dorm room, an apartment, a friend's house in which you spend all your time or your favorite couch in the library that you frequent for naps? Maybe you've set up a home already, but it's filled with the chaos of small children, busy schedules, and lack of routine. How do we carry out the Christian call to welcome the stranger when our homes are such fragmented and chaotic spaces?

Below we will examine some hospitable practices in which we can embody Christ's welcome and connect the ministry of the church wherever life might take us. These practices not only create space for others in our Christian journey but also give us space to reflect and examine our place in the church as we bring the ministry of the church outside the church walls and into our lives.

ACTS OF HOSPITALITY ARE NOT BLACKMAIL OR FIGURES IN A KIND OF POLITICAL CALCULATION BUT RATHER A WAY OF ESTABLISHING AND REMEMBERING WHAT KIND OF DISTINCTIVE PEOPLE WE ARE AS CHRISTIANS.

As part of a younger generation looking for a place in the church, these practices are part of the prophetic presence that reveal how and where the kingdom of God is breaking into our congregations. By engaging in these practices, we hope that young people will be able to offer the gift of their presence to the church and, when necessary, ask boldly for hospitality to be extended in return. Hospitality, of course, is not a technique to gain acceptance or a strategy to be used against others. Nor is it a practice that can demand or except reciprocity, because it is a gift freely given. Rather, it is a genuine welcome of the other, a welcome that first requires that technique and strategy be set aside. Acts of hospitality, in other words, are not blackmail. They are not figures in a kind of political calculation but rather a way of establishing and remembering what kind of distinctive people we are as Christians. This, we think, must first be established by engendering what we call a "peaceable presence."

## PEACEABLE PRESENCE

The kind of peaceable presence we have in mind is the kind that can't be found in *O, Martha Stewart Living,* or *Better Homes and Gardens,* because true hospitality is focused on welcoming others rather than entertaining or making the right impression.

This is where so many of us get off track when it comes to hospitality. Because our society assumes hospitality is entertainment or impression-making, the mere thought of hosting often creates anxiety. "When hospitality is viewed as entertainment," Pohl writes, "the house is never ready."[2] Worries about appearances and presentation often override attentiveness to the greater needs of others.

Especially for those of us who are in our twenties, the thought of playing host to someone in our church who is older and more established can be about as peaceful as a fork to the eye. We think about the hospitality that has been extended to us by older generations at our church near Chicago. Their homes are beautifully decorated, and their decades of culinary experience show with every dish presented at the dinner table. They have the right china, beautiful silver, and the right detail in every aspect of the meal. Our dining room has white walls. The extent of our china collection is one place setting that we received as a wedding gift (and is still in the box). Usually, the welcome includes our dog immediately and rudely invading our guests' sense of personal space. Our ability to extend hospitality is very different from what older, more established generations can usually do.

It's not that we think extending hospitality should be a miserable experience but one that is marked by a peaceable presence in which anxiety over not having the right silverware isn't given a place. Hospitality is a genuine welcome, which means that while we extend good gifts, we strive for welcome rather than perfection in the finest aspects of entertaining.

Anxiety cannot create a hospitable posture, one in which guests experience the very peace of Christ. If you've ever been offered hospitality by a host who is overly concerned with the presentation of entertainment, you probably have a good idea of what we're talking about.

Anxiety about hospitality often reflects the deeper sense of fragmentation we have about life in general.

A non-anxious presence is being deeply connected with a person or persons in our company while being detached from the stress and emotions brought on by outside elements. This practice is deeply spiritual and forms us to be a people who are not restless about the things of this world but have found rest in God, as Augustine would say. Jesus told us to consider the flowers of the field. If God clothes them with such beauty, how much more will God clothe and care for us (Matthew 6:28-29)?

When we encounter others who are harried by the brokenness of their lives, we can enter into their brokenness and sit alongside them without perpetuating the same anxiety they have over the situation, because we know the One who cares for every need. In the process, we create an environment in which this friend or stranger can also find true rest and welcome.

One of our favorite examples of this was demonstrated in the lives of some dear friends who, while being a few years older than us, are still people we would consider as being in our generation. Whatever their age, they're who we think of when we imagine hosts who extend a peaceable presence in their hospitality. They have a fantastic house filled with the signs of life: crayons, toys, clothes, a tired old dog, and a wall painted with chalkboard paint for their four kids to express their artistic side. There is nothing about their home that would suggest that kids don't live there, but more wonderfully yet, there's nothing they do to try to hide that fact. When you are welcomed into their home, it's a genuine welcome, and we love receiving their hospitality.

That welcome was also extended to some strangers one evening when Beth, who had invited another couple to drop their kids at the house so they could have a night out, forgot to mention it to her husband, Brian. When the doorbell rang, Brian opened the door to find several children and a smiling mother on the porch. He hadn't met any of them before, didn't know their names, and didn't know they were coming over. "Welcome—guests!" he exclaimed, hoping that the euphemistic pronoun he used wasn't too obvious. "Kids, come out here and say hello to our guests!" Maybe Brian didn't have any other possibilities in that situation, but we love the fact that his default reaction was that of hospitality. If his extension of hospitality to us is any indicator, it's our suspicion that his welcome of some unexpected guests was a welcome that didn't worry all that much about what the house looked like or whether or not the kids had picked up their toys. When we think about a welcome that's established without anxiety in a peaceable presence, this is what comes to our minds.

AT HOME, WORK, SCHOOL, OR OUT ON THE TOWN, CHRISTIANS CAN PRACTICE HOSPITALITY BY OFFERING A NON-ANXIOUS, PEACEABLE PRESENCE TO STRANGERS IN NEED OF REST.

At home, work, school, or out on the town, Christians can practice hospitality by offering a non-anxious, peaceable presence to strangers in need of rest. You don't have to offer them a couch and a cup of tea—although if you have those things to offer, go right ahead! You can't create a hospitable environment with candles and doilies alone. Rather, it's when your peaceable presence welcomes people to experience the respite and welcome Christ offers to all who are weary and in need of healing and redemption.

How many times have you entered a party or a home of someone else, taken a deep breath before crossing through the door, plastered on a fake smile, and told yourself, "Here we go again"? How many times have you entered church feeling the same way? But every now and then we enter those places where we have true friends, where we understand that no facade is needed. What if you could be that presence for others? What if you could begin to cultivate that in your church?

Churches ought to be a true sanctuary where the weary can enter and find rest. But they are so often harried by the many activities and events, meetings, and obligations. For those of us who have grown up in the church, we know just how demanding and stressful church life can be. But where is the rest that Christ offers? Being a peaceable presence amidst the business of church life can have a prophetic witness to your brothers and sisters hurriedly going about the business of church without encountering the spirit of peace.

One of our youth sponsors came back from winter retreat, as most adults return from a youth event, exhausted and infected with the illness *de jour*, compliments of our beloved but grossly unsanitized teenagers. She was deeply weary, not only from the weekend but from life in general. She felt as if she hadn't seen her husband in weeks and didn't know how she was ever going to overcome the mountain of laundry that had amassed at her house. Inviting her into our home filled with the sounds of a screaming baby was probably not the most restful experience we could offer her, nor would it help with the laundry pile. Instead, we quietly listened to her to-do list and offered to cover her responsibilities at youth group that week to give her an evening at home with her husband. Taking on those responsibilities didn't feel like extra work or obligation—it felt like giving a gift.

Hospitality means there are times in which creating a space of welcome and rest involves making space in the life of the other, of opening a place of renewal that is free from anxiety. That is, it is offering them that which will give them renewal and making room for redemption.

Though the home is a central location of hospitality being offered and received, being a non-anxious presence is a practice of Christian hospitality that can go with you anywhere. The more we practice the peace of Christ, the greater the gift we have to offer in our welcome to others.

## SHARING MEALS

Another act of hospitality that can extend welcome to the other is the shared meal. The modern dichotomy between hospitality and social services leaves much to be wanted in terms of actual Christian fellowship. Hospitality is for sale at restaurants and hotels where customers can enjoy their meal or bed and keep their encounter with strangers at a minimum. Meanwhile, social services like soup kitchens and shelters provide these accommodations free of charge, but clients are asked to take a number, show an ID, and sit alone. Personhood is lost in the very system and structures put in place for personal well-being.

The Christian practice of the shared meal shatters this dichotomy and invades the idea that we live our lives in separate spheres with visions of the kingdom of God. In the shared meal, strangers are invited to sit at a table of friends. Fellowship is extended beyond the boundaries of similar people groups to image the diversity and particularity of God's creation. When Christians limit the sharing of food to a social service model, we leave indelible scars on Christ's body. One example of such scars can be seen in the story of a young woman we will call Tess.

Tess is a student we worked with in a previous ministry assignment. She's quiet, desperately shy, keeps mostly to herself, and likes it that way. Whether it's her shy nature or the fact that she doesn't spend much time with others, she seems to care very little for the way she is perceived by others. Tess is one of those students who are a bit more difficult to truly welcome. Some students seize the welcome of others and instantly become part of the community. Others take more time and effort. Tess was a near impossibility.

One year Tess participated in something called a "poverty meal," which is a simulated experience aimed at visualizing the disparity of income and unjust food distribution in our world. Those who participate are separated into four different groups, each meant to represent a global economic class of people according to percentages that correlate with global statistics on world hunger. The first group has the largest number of students. They are crammed into a small square designated by duct tape on the floor. Most of them have to stand; a few are able to sit cross-legged. They are given one bowl of water and one cup filled with rice and beans to share among themselves. The next group has a few less students and is in a slightly larger duct tape square. They are given a larger supply of water, a large bowl of rice and a large bowl of beans and a few cups to divide it up. It's not a pretty meal, but there is enough to go around. The third group has even fewer students who sit at a modest table with chairs. There is a family-style meal laid out before them, and they have the option of water or iced tea to drink and several dishes of food. There is more than enough for everyone to have their fill. The fourth group has only three or four students. They are served by a wait staff and have multiple options of food as the meal is brought to them in courses. The groups aren't allowed to share food with other groups and cannot cross the borders that have been established.

As you can imagine, it's often a difficult experience for the students to act out the disparity they already participate in every day, only with fewer spectators and less guilt. But in one of these poverty meals, something very difficult indeed took place. The leader of the experience announced that one student would be allowed to move from the first group to the fourth group, but that the student would need to be chosen by his or her peers to make the move. A chair was set up off to the side of the beautifully decorated and linen-clad table as whoever its occupant would be would not be allowed to join the fourth group at the table, but would sit at a distance and eat their leftovers.

Sitting silently among the members of the first group, Tess's face bore no expression, and her eyes were locked on the floor in front of her. After much deliberation, her group decided that she would be the one to make the move to the table overflowing with hot, delicious food. She was so very thin, the group reasoned, so she must need the food the most. When the decision was made, no one asked Tess if she would like to go, but she solemnly stood, took her place in the chair and quietly accepted a paper plate filled with leftovers from the banquet table. For perhaps the first time in her life, every eye in the room was on her.

"This isn't fair," one of the occupants of the fourth group protested to the leader. "She can eat with us. There's plenty of room." He motioned to the lavish table. But the louder their protests became, the more attention was called to Tess and the more uncomfortable she became. Finally, accepting that the truth of the simulation required that she not sit with them at the table, one of the group members passed her a fork, and she began to eat her meal without a word, tears beginning to stream down her cheeks.

A stunned silence fell over the room. No one knew what to do or how to comfort her. Perhaps the students had assumed that since Tess did not seem to want their fellowship at any of their previous gatherings she would not mind being made to sit in that isolated chair. Perhaps they thought she would appreciate the food more than she would want to be included in the conversation, making her the perfect candidate for this upgrade at the poverty meal. For whatever the reason, no one saw her reaction coming. It was as if it was simply too painful for her social isolation to become part of the group demonstration on display for all to see. We remember painfully thinking, *Are we just now seeing the way Tess has been feeling every time we gather and she goes off and sits by herself? How could we have missed it? How could I have missed it?*

Tess's vulnerability before us became a prophetic presence, but unfortunately it was a role she neither sought nor desired. She didn't ask for the scars this encounter would leave any more than the poor of Israel asked to be devoured like bread (Psalm 14, 53). Her tears revealed the mockery we had unwittingly made of Christian fellowship.

Scripture tells us that we do not live on bread alone but on every word that comes from the mouth of God (Deuteronomy 8:3; Matthew 4:4; Luke 4:4). And if you'll allow us a little theological and literary liberty, we also remember that the Word became flesh and made His dwelling among us (John 1:14), suggesting that beyond the mere nutrients of bread, we also starve for the Word of God, which became flesh and made His dwelling with us, in fellowship, communion, and hospitality, sharing meals, eating with sinners, welcoming the outsiders.

How many more like Tess are out there, starving for the fellowship of Christ's Body? How might sharing a meal open the opportunity for those like Tess—who are so often on the outside in their own isolation—and begin to open a place for them in the fellowship of Christ's Body? How might literally making a place for them at the table signal to them that Christ's welcome extends to them as well? For those who wonder if they have a place in the church, breaking bread together will usually answer that question in the affirmative.

Sharing a meal with someone is about much more than merely ingesting calories and absorbing nutrients, as important as that may be, lest we forget how many of our brothers and sisters go without this basic need. But sharing a meal is a time when Christians unmask the false dichotomy of consumer hospitality and social services by witnessing to the kingdom of God in something as ordinary as breaking bread. It is a practice in which the fragmentation of our lives can be healed by fellowship with other members of

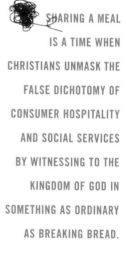

SHARING A MEAL IS A TIME WHEN CHRISTIANS UNMASK THE FALSE DICHOTOMY OF CONSUMER HOSPITALITY AND SOCIAL SERVICES BY WITNESSING TO THE KINGDOM OF GOD IN SOMETHING AS ORDINARY AS BREAKING BREAD.

Christ's Body, where we can reclaim one another from isolation and open a place for them at the table.

Of course, Christians have been sharing meals together since there have been Christians. It was Christ himself who instituted this practice of hospitality when He took bread, blessed it, broke it, and gave it to His disciples, saying, "This is my body, given for you" (Matthew 26:26, Mark 14:22, Luke 22:19). The practice continued as sharing full meals together in the Early Church, making the Lord's Supper the central point of gathering for Christians. In other words, when Christians gathered for worship, food was shared.

It is in sharing the bread of Christ's body, in receiving His hospitality, that we together become the Body of Christ. The Lord's Supper is far more than an act of individual introspection and repentance, but it is also a shared meal at which all who desire to be near Jesus have a place and are established together as God's redemption people. It is a meal where isolation and fragmentation give way to the grace of being welcomed into a community that gathers in the name of Christ, a community of redeemed and healed people.

For those who are wondering if there is a seat for them at the table, we answer *yes*. Christ himself has already made that place available to you by giving himself to be the food around which we gather. Our own practices of hospitality, of sharing meals together and breaking bread, are helpful to us in remembering this reality and living into the reality that we are not fragmented and isolated, like Tess so poignantly reminded us, but that we are invited to the table to feast on the grace of God and to leave forever transformed.

When one eats alone, it stands as a powerful prophetic presence to the church that we have not broken bread right. It was the practice of eating meals together that exposed the divisions in the Corinthian church, breaking Paul's heart as he wrote to them, "I hear that when you come together as a church, there are divisions among you, and to some extent I believe it. No doubt there have to be differences among you to show which of you have God's approval. So then, when you come together, it is not the Lord's Supper you eat" (1 Corinthians 11:18-20).

Those differences of which he speaks, rooted in the idea that God approves of some and not others, brings to light the inhospitable practices of having a meal and not making space for those who are on the outside. It shows us when our communion is broken, for when there are those among us who remain hungry (1 Corinthians 11:21) for a taste of God's grace, our body is not functioning as it was designed to function.

Sharing meals not only makes a place for those who wonder if they have a place in the church; it also serves as a way for us to examine ourselves as the church and ask if there are some who aren't able to find space at the feast, and then do the humble and healing work of asking what we might be able to do to welcome those who desire a seat at the table.

## SHARING COMMITMENTS AND PRACTICES

If you've read through Leviticus lately (yeah, right) you probably noticed some pretty interesting laws. From farming to foreskin, mildew to menstruation, every part of life for the ancient Israelites was called into a particular and peculiar set of practices. These shared practices served to establish the boundaries that marked the Israelites' community as God's chosen people and identified their difference from the world around them. This might sound exclusivist and smug, but before we write off these peculiar practices it might help to talk a bit about the concept of difference.

Over the last century, some philosophers have clued into the idea that humanity tends to try and assimilate anything or anyone who is different into the dominant culture.[3] When we look at another who is different, we see an illogical version of ourselves and disregard the person's particularity. What this does is essentially homogenizes us and dismisses the particularity that is necessary for communion, as we talked about a few chapters earlier.

Difference, though, is one of the two key ingredients of Christian communion. When difference among humans is mixed with submission to Christ's lordship, Christian community is the incredible result. One of the things we've loved about our churches over the years is that there were so many people who were pretty different from us. Sure, it would be easier sometimes if everyone thought the way we did or saw the same side of every issue, but that wouldn't be authentic community. The beauty of it all was that, rather than becoming overly suspicious of other people's motivations for holding a different opinion on an issue, we could always rely on the fact that they, too, had submitted their lives to Christ's leading and that their viewpoint was most likely the way in which they saw the best way of living faithfully to Christ. The point is that Christian communities need some amount of difference within them to function. Without difference or distance we cannot welcome the other, because we don't know where I end and the other begins, and the whole thing begins to collapse into homogeneity. If you remember the example of the softball team from chapter 7, you know that we have to have unity—but not homogeneity. There is a certain sense of particularity that needs to be present for communities to function.

So what does any of this have to do with hospitality? As we've tried to establish so far, Christian communities ought to be places of welcome. But they need to be distinctive communities so that there is a clear space into which the outsider is welcomed. We should ask things like "Who are we, and why is our community worth the welcome?" Or in other words, if there is nothing different about the Christian community, why bother trying to welcome someone in?

In the same way that there needs to be some amount of difference between people to maintain a community, there also needs to be some amount of difference that sets the community apart from the rest of the world, and part of that difference would be the practices of our community that make us distinct in some way.

Let's go back to the example of the softball team for a moment. What makes a softball team a softball team? It's that they do different things from all the other communities out there. They get together in specific softball times and specific softball places and do specific softball things. Or another way of saying it is that they share common practices. When someone wants to join a softball team, that person can experience the joy of softball only by joining in the specific practices that the softball team shares together. Because if these practices aren't shared—if one person comes to bowl, another to golf, and another to play badminton—there are no longer shared practices that make the softball team a distinct community that is able to welcome other lovers of softball. Just think about what it might be like for you to invite a friend to join your softball team and when she arrives she finds each member of the team in a different corner of the field with different sporting instruments: fishing poles, badminton rackets, snowboards, and so on. The experience would be miserable for her, not to mention bizarre, and she would never get to experience the joy of playing softball. If she is going to be truly welcome, the community needs to share some common practices.

The church, too, is a specific community that gathers in specific places at specific times to do specific things. In other words, it is a distinct community that lives according to God's grace in the name of Christ through the Holy Spirit's empowerment. Something like a softball team, shared practices mark out the distinct boundaries into which we can welcome others. If everyone shows up to church but never shares any practices, it becomes difficult for us to welcome others into our communion. But to provide welcome there must be shared practices that mark out difference.

WE ENCOURAGE CHURCHES TO BE THE KINDS OF COMMUNITIES THAT SHARE PRACTICES TOGETHER BECAUSE THOSE PRACTICES ARE WHAT MAKE THE CHURCH DISTINCT.

With this in mind, we encourage churches to be the kinds of communities that share practices together because those practices are what make the church distinct and thus a community into which we can welcome others. The life and love shared among the community becomes the fluid space into which strangers, sinners, and broken people are invited to rest and meet Jesus. If these communities hope to provide that place of welcome, there must be shared practices that make these communities marked out as distinct from their groups and gatherings by their shared commitments and practices that speak to their character. Practices that are particular, that set boundaries for the particular community of the church, are many, and we can't say what they should be for each church, but they ought to be distinct, growing out of a commitment to God's mission of redemption and healing in the world. Once the community has been defined by those shared practices, it can become a place of warm welcome to those who are seeking a place in that community of God's redemption.

When I (Shawna) was a teenager, I would say some inane thing to my parents such as "But Lisa's parents let her play in the Sunday soccer league!" My parents would coolly reply, "Yes, and we are not Lisa's parents." My family had practices that made us different.

For instance, a family holds to certain practices and commitments, such as the television set remaining off until chores and homework are done, keeping the toilet seat down so the dog doesn't drink out of it, dinner at six o'clock, no phones at the dinner table, and so on. These rules or practices create a shared experience of life where members know what to expect and how to best interact with others to keep peace and unity.

For those who have moved out of seemingly restrictive communities (also known as your parents' home or college dorms) in a relatively recent timeframe, submitting to the practices of another community might not sound particularly appealing. Perhaps you're thinking, *I'm wondering if I have a place in the church, not in a boot camp.* But we would like to suggest that engaging those shared practices can actually be an incredibly freeing move. In joining the shared practices of the church, or even discerning what kinds of practices God may be asking you to institute in the church, there is a sense in which the members of the community are free to exhibit the membership of that community. Like the family shared practices, if the practices set the tone, a sense of stability is often the result. And a stable community is one that is poised to offer a welcome. In what seems to be a paradox, those communities (like families) that have clear practices are those who have the clearest sense of who they are and thus are able to welcome others into their midst in a non-anxious way, offering a peaceable presence to the outsider. Again, we think of those times we have been hosted by someone who was constantly adjusting his or her decorations, food, drink, or even opinions and way of speech according to what he or she thought we expected, and those memories are all associated with a distinct sense of anxiety. Shared practices, however, serve to set up a clear sense of identity so that our welcome is genuine according to the distinctive difference of our community.

Our church in San Diego had a strong sense of identity formed by shared practices. We prayed in our services—a lot. We ate together once a week over Bible study—hungry people from all walks of life were welcome. We had members sing "special music" each week, and they were sometimes hard to listen to. We received Communion every service. One Sunday Tim's roommate asked if it would be a problem if he tagged along with him to church. Knowing that this roommate was a musician and had a discerning taste in music, Tim was a bit anxious about what would be waiting for them at church. When the special music rolled around, it was an a capella rendition of a song by a woman in the congregation who gave it everything she had. Whether it was the singularly most beautiful version wasn't really the point. It was a true testimony. Tim knew, though, that it would probably be the last time his roommate would ever make it to church with him.

To his surprise, he looked at his roommate and noticed he was visibly moved by the song. "It was real," he remembers his roommate saying after the service. "She meant every word." The next week Tim's roommate made the trip to church with him, and the week after that, and the week after that. There was something authentic about the shared practices of the community that was able to offer a non-anxious, peaceable welcome to a young man who found his place among the shared practices of a Christ-centered community.

It is increasingly difficult to submit to external practices and commitments. The more we praise individual uniqueness and esteeming oneself highly, the more difficult it becomes for us to imagine that something outside ourselves could actually be better than anything we possess on our own. This seems to be particularly true for the YouTube generation, whose public school curriculum included things like self-esteem training. James Davidson Hunter's book *Death of Character: Morality in an Age without Good and Evil*, gives a terrific analysis of the American school system's evolution over the last two hundred years as educators have attempted to instill character in children.[4] He comes to the conclusion that as schools and society at large attempted to teach character without giving any bias to a particular sect or creed but rather appealing to a universal set of moral principles, they became impotent to enact any true character formation and settled instead for an empty morality.

Tim sees the same thing taking shape in many of the college students who take his ethics course. Ethics deals with measuring the goodness of a particular action, but increasingly, students are unable to engage in this kind of analysis because they aren't sure what goodness is. They are suspicious of ancient ways of thinking ethically, because philosophers like Plato and Aristotle argued that you must first be aware that there is an objective Good, and then you can shape your action or character according to that Good. In the absence of that Good, however, students are left stumbling around to attempt to prove that a particular act or character trait is good.

Usually, when pushed to define why something is good, it comes back to how it happens to make them feel about it in that moment, or a vague sense of politeness or niceness. It is almost as if they are like people who have never seen color, attempting to describe the hue of the sky. The character that is formed within them, then, is the kind of character that is measured not by any external criteria but by their feelings about themselves.

Character can't be shaped in abstraction if it is going to be character. There must be an external correlate, a community whose concrete practices reflect a particular creed that makes a community different. In the absence of such external correlation, or without the special practices of a community that form a distinctive character, we aren't really sure if we can say that something is good or not.

Shared practices help us know who we are. They form character deeply within us, unifying and uniting persons, establishing them into a community of particularity. And once character is so formed, the church community can be a place where those who are wondering if there is a place for them can be invited in to the communion, find a place at the table,

THE CHURCH COMMUNITY CAN BE A PLACE WHERE THOSE WHO ARE WONDERING IF THERE IS A PLACE FOR THEM CAN BE INVITED IN TO THE COMMUNION, FIND A PLACE AT THE TABLE, AND REST IN THE PEACEABLE PRESENCE OF A PEOPLE WHO KNOW DEEPLY THAT JESUS CHRIST IS THEIR LORD.

and rest in the peaceable presence of a people who know deeply that Jesus Christ is their Lord.

## ATTENTIVE SPACE

Finally, hospitable places are spaces that are attentive to the needs of others. What would hospitality be if it offered much that was not needed? Your car can be an attentive place when it is stocked with bottles of water and small packets of sunscreen during a hot summer and warm blankets and mittens in the winter. Your home can be an attentive place when its resources can be easily allocated to confront the need of a surprise guest who is without a place for the evening. Your church, too, can be an attentive space by engaging in hospitable practices of listening, watching, and learning from those who are strangers and aliens.

An adjustment in the kinds of ministry the church offers does not change God's mission of redemption and healing in the world. We spoke with members of a church board about a new outreach activity they recently attempted. Their church housed a large food pantry, which let them know their city was filled with families of various ethnicities who were in need of supplies for their pantries. Still, they were struggling to reach this community. When we asked what they were doing in terms of outreach, they told us about a recent ballroom dancing class they had offered. "No one showed up but us church members," they said honestly, "but we had a good time." Ballroom dancing may not have been indicative of an attentive space. If the church is to engage in mission, if it is to be included in what God is doing in the world, it must have the eyes to see and the ears to hear the surprising way God is redeeming this world.

Imagine the absurdity of entering a place of hospitality on a brutally hot day and being offered a coat, a blanket, and a cup of hot tea. It seems to go without saying that practices of attentive hospitality would stop these kinds of things before they take place, but how often do we measure the church's level of attentive hospitality? Especially when it comes to those who are wondering if they have a place in the church, what might practices of attentive hospitality be able to offer those who wonder if they have a seat at the table? Are we attentive to the needs of those who are outsiders? Or are we content to continue to offer the same kind of hospitality, no matter what the need? What might it take to offer a place at the table to someone who wonders if he or she is welcome at the table to begin with?

It is our sincere hope that a serious and sustained conversation and attention to the Christian tradition of offering hospitality would be a hopeful reminder that young people have a place in the church, that there is room at the table for their particularity. Sometimes there is a prophetic nature to hospitality in that we must come asking boldly for it to be extended to us.

But in coming with bold expectations, we are also hopeful for the church, that as the Spirit continues to sharpen the church's hospitable senses, the idea of a person eating whatever falls from our overflowing table would be an image strong enough to bring about a change of practice and a deep desire to make space at the table for those who long to be invited to the banquet.

# CONCLUSION
## COFFEE WITH PAPA

THIS YEAR at Thanksgiving there was no oyster stuffing on the table. In fact, nothing that was on the table came as a surprise. The steadiness of long-held family tradition brought us those expertly prepared dishes that have been present at every family holiday meal that Shawna can remember. There wasn't an oyster in sight.

Holiday meals with Shawna's family are always a big occasion. Relatives from both sides of the family get together, we borrow extra chairs and tables from the church, and everyone eats more ham and cheesy corn casserole than ought to be legal. After the meal, we make coffee and have dessert and sit around the house in a calorie-induced coma. After the coffee is poured and the pie is sliced, it's time to forge solutions to all the world's problems. And we usually do a pretty good job of it—if we do say so ourselves. If only the United Nations would ask us for help.

This year we sat down around the table, coffee in one hand, Mema's famous apple pie in the other. With a look of great unease and seriousness in his voice, Papa looked at us and asked, "Have you heard about this new church called 'emergent'?"

We had. Many of our friends in college and seminary had been impacted by the ministry of churches that had either taken on the label of "emergent" willingly or had it placed upon them by others. We had also heard about all the controversy surrounding "emergent" churches and had seen how deeply our friends had been hurt by it. Sometimes they were called heretics.

Were the charges of heresy valid in some cases? Possibly. But more often than flat-out attempts at making heretical claims, the "emergent" churches that we knew of had become places where young Christians had gathered together and began asking tough questions about faith that often had no easy answers. Many of them felt as if their questions had no place in the larger church, that their questioning had cost them a seat at the table. As they attempted to find answers to their questions, controversy began to swirl around these churches, and the same kinds of generational divides marked by confusion, suspicion, and blogospheric vitriol began to surface.

It seems that the emergent church is one of those things that nearly every person in or around the church has an opinion about, but if we could ask you to put your feelings about these churches on hold for a moment, you'll see that our purpose of telling this story is not to wade into the particular debate over whether the emergent church is a faithful or heretical movement, mainly because there are so few officially coordinated practices and views shared by churches who call themselves emergent. We don't happen to think that anyone and anything that has been labeled "emergent" is automatically heretical, nor do we hold that emergent churches are the sole future and salvation of the Christian faith. Wherever the gospel of Christ is being faithfully proclaimed, we say thanks be to God. Wherever the church has erred, we pray for her healing.

We tell this story, however, to provide an example of how distance between the generations can lead to division in the church and leave young people feeling placeless—or how that doesn't always have to be the reality.

Papa went on to describe what he had heard about this new kind of church and how it was leading young people astray with heretical doctrine and all manner of practices that were foreign to faithful Christian worship. In hearing his description, Papa clearly thought that "emergent" was a fixed body of people who all agreed that the Virgin Birth was a bunch of bunk, played fast and loose with Scripture, and were out to destroy the church.

This was one of those conversations that could have ended very badly. In the backs of our minds we heard echoes of many of our friends recounting stories of similar conversations that ended with someone storming out of the room, leaving the church—or worse, leaving the faith altogether.

We were also acutely aware that when confusion or suspicion enters a world of dualisms, it usually means that one party will be left with no choice but to consider the other party's faith broken in some way. I don't think we could begin to describe how pained we would be if Papa was suspicious that our faith in Christ was somehow defective or heretical, and so we were pretty quiet for a while.

While we weren't certain that the fears Papa had about these churches applied to every congregation that has taken on or been given the "emergent" title, while we listened to his concerns, we became exceedingly certain that everything Papa shared with us was with the utmost sincerity and genuine concern for the youth of the church. We were also certain that he didn't want to see us swayed by something that he understood to be contrary to the good news of Christ that had so deeply marked his life.

Instead of the conflict we dreaded, a wonderful conversation unfolded over coffee and pie that night. We came to a deeper understanding that Papa and Mema were part of a generation who had spilled sweat, blood, and tears laying a solid foundation for the church to nurture future generations in Christ's love. They had given their lives to the church, not because it was their duty or obligation but because they knew they were former sinners saved by grace and wanted nothing but grace upon grace for their children and grandchildren. If they did feel a sense of duty, it was to their Creator and Savior.

Any reasons they were given to suspect that something or someone was leading a younger generation astray was heartbreaking to them, even filling them with righteous anger. To our betterment and blessing, we got to know Papa and Mema a little better that night.

Papa and Mema also got to know us a little better that same night. We, too, are sinners saved by grace. And we see our Savior who came to us in flesh to offer us grace as a clear call and charge to find where the kingdom of God is breaking into our world, even in the midst of our culture, and join the good work God is doing. Words like "duty" may not carry as much weight with our generation, but when Christians our age catch a glimpse of the wideness of God's mission, we tend to get a little passionate and maybe even dedicate ourselves to follow Christ wherever He may lead.

We would like to think that the conversation with Papa that night was one of the "holy conversations" we've talked about in this book. Our talk with Papa over coffee took place in the context of the trust, love, and knowledge that we both wanted to remain faithful. Though Papa may have been a bit perplexed by the expressions of faith from our generation, our conversation didn't dissolve into suspicion of each other. Before the question was asked, we knew that Papa's first concern was faithfulness to Jesus Christ. Before we could add cream and sugar to our cups, Papa knew that we put Christ before all other commitments or cultural assumptions. There was no need to enter into a conversation with our guard up and suspicions high. We had prayed for and with each other. We had shared meals together. We had given and received hospitality. We knew each other.

Perhaps this is the reason Paul so closely relates knowledge and love in his letter to the Corinthian church. Maybe he, too, saw that love is a close companion of intimate knowledge of another person, even a person in another generation. "Love never fails," he reminds the Corinthian Christians (1 Corinthians 13:8). "It always protects, always trusts, always hopes, always perseveres" (verse 7). But that love, for Paul, is tied closely to knowledge. "Now I know in part," he writes only a few verses later, "then I shall know fully, even as I am fully known" (1 Corinthians 13:12).

To know God is to be known by God. To love God is to be loved by God. They are one in the same. But the knowledge of God is often imparted through relationships, especially with those who have been known by God for a long time. Our conversation with Papa that night helped us to know God a bit better and to be known by God in return. In other words, we were finding a seat at the table.

If you have struggled to find a place in the church, if you are wondering if there is room for you, we hope you will allow yourself to know and be known. The confusion and suspicion that so often accompany difference are rarely maintained in the face of deep, relational knowledge. Give yourself to knowing, and allow yourself to be known in return. You may just find that the distance between generations is not an impossible impasse—and that a welcome is not as far off as you once thought.

A welcome was not as far away as the Gentile woman in Matthew 15 may have thought. Feeling as much like an outsider as anyone could, she came to Jesus, hoping for a small bit of what He was bringing in its wholeness. Jesus' disciples wanted her to be sent away. In their eyes, she did not have a place among them. And yet she came to Jesus anyway, falling down before Him in great faith and asking for His healing. As much as we don't like seeing echoes of this story in the church we love so much, we recognize that they are present and that there are those among us who are truly wondering if the church has a place for them.

It's our sincere hope that this book offered a source of hope and some practical, theologically valid practices for those who are either wondering if there is a place for them in the church or if their churches are the kinds of communities that naturally make room for young people to come to know Christ. We also hope that the stories contained in this volume and the subsequent reflections upon them serve to encourage where encouragement is needed and challenge where challenge is necessary. Ultimately, however, we deeply desire for the church to faithfully accept its role as a sign and symbol of the kingdom of God.

We know that there are many more stories to be told. We know that the particularity of the stories we included in this book may not express every viewpoint or touch on every issue. But we hope they have offered a kind of approach to life in the church that seeks to listen deeply to what is happening in particular contexts and to try to discern from those stories how the church might be more and more faithful to its calling. There are many more theological tools we weren't able to use in this book, but we hope for those who have encountered them that they will seek out more tools that the Christian theological tradition offers to us to help the church be more and more faithful to its calling.

Is there a place for young people at the table? Is the YouTube generation simply resigned to leaving the church because there is no place for them? We don't think so. We're hopeful, in fact, that God is at work in the young generation and that this is a generation who may very well be involved in God's healing of this creation. If you still wonder if the church has a place for you at the table, though, we hope that your encounter with this book has not only given some amount of hope that the above questions can be answered in the affirmative, but also that an affirmative answer is given to us because of the kind of community the church is.

Called by God to be an image of the divine and agents of God's mission of healing and redemption, the church is that unique body that assembles under Christ's lordship and in our particularity. Assembled from different backgrounds and holding different views of the world but serving one Lord, the church is a place of hospitality for those who desire to receive the gifts of God. In the story of the Gentile woman in Matthew 15, we learn that the Kingdom expands to outsiders, that the redemption and healing to be found in the Kingdom are available not only to those who are inside but also to those who long for a seat at the table. We hope that this book in some small way helps the church meet its calling by making a place at the table for the young generation.

# NOTES

## INTRODUCTION

1. Robert D. Putnam and David E. Campbell, *American Grace: How Religion Divides and Unites Us* (New York: Simon & Schuster, 2010); and Lisa D. Pearce and Melinda Lundquist Denton, *A Faith of Their Own: Stability and Change in the Religiosity of America's Adolescents* (New York: Oxford University Press, 2011).

## CHAPTER 1

1. Putnam and Campbell, *American Grace*, 123.
2. The Barna Group, Ltd. YouthPollSM 1995-2006.
3. Putnam and Campbell, *American Grace*, 80 ff.
4. Ibid., 82.
5. Drew Dyck, "The Leavers: Young Doubters Exit the Church," in *Christianity Today*, November 2010.
6. David Kinnaman, *You Lost Me: Why Young Christians Are Leaving the Church . . . and Rethinking Faith* (Grand Rapids: Baker Books, 2011), 11.

## CHAPTER 2

1. Jeffrey Jensen Arnett, *Emerging Adulthood: The Winding Road from the Late Teens through the Twenties* (Oxford, England: Oxford University Press, 2006), 173.
2. Sonja Steptoe-Bellflower, "In Touch with Jesus," in *Time*, October 31, 2006.
3. Christian Smith with Melinda Lundquist Duncan, *Soul Searching: The Religious and Spiritual Lives of American Teenagers* (Oxford, England: Oxford University Press, 2005), 269.
4. Ibid., 118-71.
5. Ibid., 43.

## CHAPTER 3

1. John Wesley, "The New Birth," in *The Works of John Wesley* (Grand Rapids: Baker Books, 2002), 6:66.
2. Ibid., 67.
3. Barry Schwartz, T*he Paradox of Choice: Why More Is Less* (New York: HarperCollins, 2004).
4. Ibid.
5. Wesley, 6:71-72.

## CHAPTER 4

1. Immanuel Kant, *Critique of Pure Reason*, in Paul Guyer and Allen W. Wood, ed. (Cambridge, England: Cambridge University Press, 1998), 121.

## CHAPTER 5

1. Putnam and Campbell, *American Grace,* 421.

2. Augustine, *Confessions*, trans. Henry Chadwick (Oxford, England: Oxford University Press, 2008), 29 ff.

3. Ibid., 3.

4. David Kinnaman, *You Lost Me: Why Young Christians Are Leaving the Church . . . and Rethinking the Faith* (Grand Rapids: Baker Books, 2011), 11.

5. Nolan M. McCarty, Keith T. Poole, and Howard Rosenthal, *Polarized America: The Dance of Ideology and Unequal Riches* (Cambridge, Mass.: Massachusetts Institute of Technology, 2006), 3 ff.

## CHAPTER 7

1. Rene Descartes, *Discourse on Method*, ed. Ian Maclean (Oxford, England: Oxford University Press, 2008), 28.

2. Robert Coles, *The Spiritual Life of Children* (Boston: Houghton Mifflin Co., 1990). Study described throughout the book.

## CHAPTER 8

1. <http://www.cbsnews.com/stories/2006/10/04/national/main2059816.shtml>.

## CHAPTER 9

1. Christine D. Phol, *Making Room: Recovering Hospitality as a Christian Tradition* (Grand Rapids: William B. Eerdmans Publishing Co., 1999), 150 ff.

2. Ibid., 154.

3. One example is found in Martin Buber, *I and Thou* (New York: Scribner, 2000). Another is Emmanuel Levinas, *Totality and Infinity: An Essay on Exteriority* (Norwell, Mass.: Kluwer Academic Publishers, 1991).

4. James Davison Hunter, *The Death of Character: Moral Education in an Age Without Good or Evil* (New York: Basic Books, 2000).